The Truth About Jesus Is He a Myth?

Mangasar Magurditch Mangasarian

Contents

THE TRUTH ABOUT JESUS
IS HE A MYTH?

BY

Mangasar Magurditch Mangasarian

By education most have been misled, So they believe because they were so bred; The priest continues what the nurse began, And thus the child imposes on the man.

DRYDEN.

PREFACE

The following work offers in book form the series of studies on the question of the historicity of Jesus, presented from time to time before the Independent Religious Society in Orchestra Hall. No effort has been made to change the manner of the spoken, into the more regular form of the written, word.

M. M. MANGASARIAN.
ORCHESTRA HALL CHICAGO

PART I.
A PARABLE

I am today twenty-five hundred years old. I have been dead for nearly as many years. My place of birth was Athens; my grave was not far from those of Xenophon and Plato, within view of the white glory of Athens and the shimmering waters of the Aegean sea.

After sleeping in my grave for many centuries I awoke suddenly--I cannot tell how nor why--and was transported by a force beyond my control to this new day and this new city. I arrived here at daybreak, when the sky was still dull and drowsy. As I approached the city I heard bells ringing, and a little later I found the streets astir with throngs of well dressed people in family groups wending their way hither and thither. Evidently they were not going to work, for they were accompanied by their children in their best clothes, and a pleasant expression was upon their faces.

"This must be a day of festival and worship, devoted to one of their gods," I murmured to myself.

Looking about me I saw a gentleman in a neat black dress, smiling, and his hand extended to me with great cordiality. He must have realized I was a stranger and wished to tender his hospitality to me. I accepted it gratefully. I clasped his hand. He pressed mine. We gazed for a moment silently into each other's eyes. He understood my bewilderment amid my novel surroundings, and offered to enlighten me. He explained to me the ringing of the bells and the meaning of the holiday crowds moving in the streets. It was Sunday--Sunday before Christmas, and the people were going to "the House of God."

"Of course you are going there, too," I said to my friendly guide.

"Yes," he answered, "I conduct the worship. I am a priest."

"A priest of Apollo?" I interrogated.

"No, no," he replied, raising his hand to command silence, "Apollo is not a god; he was only an idol."

"An idol?" I whispered, taken by surprise.

"I perceive you are a Greek," he said to me, "and the Greeks," he continued, "notwithstanding their distinguished accomplishments, were an idolatrous people. They worshipped gods that did not exist. They built temples to divinities which were merely empty names--empty names," he repeated. "Apollo and Athene--and the entire Olympian lot were no more than inventions of the fancy."

"But the Greeks loved their gods," I protested, my heart clamoring in my breast.

"They were not gods, they were idols, and the difference between a god and an idol is this: an idol is a thing; God is a living being. When you cannot prove the existence of your god, when you have never seen him, nor heard his voice, nor touched him--when you have nothing provable about him, he is an idol. Have you seen Apollo? Have you heard him? Have you touched him?"

"No," I said, in a low voice.

"Do you know of any one who has?"

I had to admit that I did not.

"He was an idol, then, and not a god."

"But many of us Greeks," I said, "have felt Apollo in our hearts and have been inspired by him."

"You imagine you have," returned my guide. "If he were really divine he would be living to this day."

"Is he, then, dead?" I asked.

"He never lived; and for the last two thousand years or more his temple has been a heap of ruins."

I wept to hear that Apollo, the god of light and music, was no more--that his fair temple had fallen into ruins and the fire upon his altar had been extinguished; then, wiping a tear from my eyes, I said, "Oh, but our gods were fair and beautiful; our religion was rich and picturesque. It made the Greeks a nation of poets, orators, artists, warriors, thinkers. It made Athens a city of light; it created the beautiful, the true, the good--yes, our religion was divine."

"It had only one fault," interrupted my guide.

"What was that?" I inquired, without knowing what his answer would be.

"It was not true."

"But I still believe in Apollo," I exclaimed; "he is not dead, I know he is alive."

"Prove it," he said to me; then, pausing for a moment, "if you produce him," he said, "we shall all fall down and worship him. Produce Apollo and he shall be our god."

"Produce him!" I whispered to myself. "What blasphemy!" Then, taking heart, I told my guide how more than once I had felt Apollo's radiant presence in my heart, and told him of the immortal lines of Homer concerning the divine Apollo. "Do you doubt Homer?" I said to him; "Homer, the inspired bard? Homer, whose inkwell was as big as the sea; whose imperishable page was Time? Homer, whose every word was a drop of light?" Then I proceeded to quote from Homer's *Iliad*, the Greek Bible, worshipped by all the Hellenes as the rarest Manuscript between heaven and earth. I quoted his description of Apollo, than whose lyre nothing is more musical, than whose speech even honey is not sweeter. I recited how his mother went from town to town to select a worthy place to give birth to the young god, son of Zeus, the Supreme Being, and how he was born and cradled amid the ministrations of all the goddesses, who bathed him in the running stream and fed him with nectar and ambrosia from Olympus. Then I recited the lines which picture Apollo bursting his bands, leaping forth from his cradle, and spreading his wings like a swan, soaring sunward, declaring that he had come to announce to mortals the will of God. "Is it possible," I asked, "that all this is pure fabrication, a fantasy of the brain, as unsubstantial as the air? No, no, Apollo is not an idol. He is a god, and the son of a god. The whole Greek world will bear me witness that I am telling the truth." Then I looked at my guide to see what impression this outburst of sincere enthusiasm had produced upon him, and I saw a cold smile upon his lips that cut me to the heart. It seemed as if he wished to say to me, "You poor deluded pagan! You are not intelligent enough to know that Homer was only a mortal after all, and that he was writing a play in which he manufactured the gods of whom he sang--that these gods existed only in his imagination, and that today they are as dead as is their inventor--the poet."

By this time we stood at the entrance of a large edifice which my guide said was "the House of God." As we walked in I saw innumerable little lights blinking and winking all over the spacious interior. There were, besides, pictures, altars and images all around me. The air was heavy with incense; a number of men in gorgeous vestments were passing to and fro, bowing and kneeling before the various lights and images. The audience was upon its knees enveloped in silence--a silence so solemn that it awed me. Observing my anxiety to understand the meaning of all this, my guide took me aside and in a whisper told me that the people were celebrating the anniversary of the birthday of their beautiful Savior--Jesus, the Son of God.

"So was Apollo the son of God," I replied, thinking perhaps that after all we might find ourselves in agreement with one another.

"Forget Apollo," he said, with a suggestion of severity in his voice. "There is no such person. He was only an idol. If you were to search for Apollo in all the universe you would never find any one answering to his name or description. Jesus," he resumed, "is the Son of God. He came to our earth and was born of a virgin."

Again I was tempted to tell my guide that that was how Apollo became incarnate; but I restrained myself.

"Then Jesus grew up to be a man," continued my guide, "performing unheard-of wonders, such as treading the seas, giving sight, hearing and speech to the blind, the deaf and the dumb, converting water into wine, feeding the multitudes miraculously, predicting coming events and resurrecting the dead."

"Of course, of your gods, too," he added, "it is claimed that they performed miracles, and of your oracles that they foretold the future, but there is this difference--the things related of your gods are a fiction, the things told of Jesus are a fact, and the difference between Paganism and Christianity is the difference between fiction and fact."

Just then I heard a wave of murmur, like the rustling of leaves in a forest, sweep over the bowed audience. I turned about and unconsciously, my Greek curiosity impelling me, I pushed forward toward where the greater candle lights were blazing. I felt that perhaps the commotion in the house was the announcement that the God Jesus was about to make his appearance, and I wanted to see him. I wanted to touch him, or, if the crowd were too large to allow me that privilege, I wanted, at least, to hear his voice. I, who had never seen a god, never touched one, never heard one speak, I who had believed in Apollo without ever having known anything provable about him, I wanted to see the real God, Jesus.

But my guide placed his hand quickly upon my shoulder, and held me back.

"I want to see Jesus," I hastened, turning toward him. I said this reverently and in good faith. "Will he not be here this morning? Will he not speak to his worshippers?" I asked again. "Will he not permit them to touch him, to caress his hand, to clasp his divine feet, to inhale the ambrosial fragrance of his breath, to bask in the golden light of his eyes, to hear the music of his immaculate accents? Let me, too, see Jesus," I pleaded.

"You cannot see him," answered my guide, with a trace of embarrassment in his voice. "He does not show himself any more."

I was too much surprised at this to make any immediate reply.

"For the last two thousand years," my guide continued, "it has not pleased Jesus to show himself to any one; neither has he been heard from for the same number of years."

"For two thousand years no one has either seen or heard Jesus?" I asked, my eyes filled with wonder and my voice quivering with excitement.

"No," he answered.

"Would not that, then," I ventured to ask, impatiently, "make Jesus as much of an idol as Apollo? And are not these people on their knees before a god of whose existence they are as much in the dark as were the Greeks of fair Apollo, and of whose past they have only rumors such as Homer reports of our Olympian gods-- as idolatrous as the Athenians? What would you say," I asked my guide, "if I were to demand that you should produce Jesus and prove him to my eyes and ears as you have asked me to produce and prove Apollo? What is the difference between a ceremony performed in honor of Apollo and one performed in honor of Jesus, since it is as impossible to give oracular demonstration of the existence of the one as of the other? If Jesus is alive and a god, and Apollo is an idol and dead, what is the evidence, since the one is as invisible, as inaccessible, and as unproducible as the other? And, if faith that Jesus is a god proves him a god, why will not faith in Apollo make him a god? But if worshipping Jesus, whom for the best part of the last two thousand years no man has seen, heard or touched; if building temples to him, burning incense upon his altars, bowing at his shrine and calling him "God," is not idolatry, neither is it idolatry to kindle fire upon the luminous altars of the Greek Apollo,--God of the dawn, master of the enchanted lyre--he with the bow and ar-row tipped with fire! I am not denying," I said, "that Jesus ever lived. He may have been alive two thousand years ago, but if he has not been heard from since, if the same thing that happened to the people living at the time he lived has happened to him, namely--if he is dead, then you are worshipping the dead, which fact stamps your religion as idolatrous."

And, then, remembering what he had said to me about the Greek mythology being beautiful but not true, I said to him: "Your temples are indeed gorgeous and costly; your music is grand; your altars are superb; your litany is exquisite; your chants are melting; your incense, and bells and flowers, your gold and silver ves-sels are all in rare taste, and I dare say your dogmas are subtle and your preachers eloquent, but your religion has one fault--***it is not true***."

IN CONFIDENCE

I shall speak in a straightforward way, and shall say today what perhaps I should say tomorrow, or ten years from now,--but shall say it today, because I cannot keep it back, because I have nothing better to say than the truth, or what I hold to be the truth. But why seek truths that are not pleasant? We cannot help it. No man can suppress the truth. Truth finds a crack or crevice to crop out of; it bobs up to the surface and all the volume and weight of waters can not keep it down. Truth prevails! Life, death, truth--behold, these three no power can keep back. And since we are doomed to know the truth, let us cultivate a love for it. It is of no avail to cry over lost illusions, to long for vanished dreams, or to call to the departing gods to come back. It may be pleasant to play with toys and dolls all our life, but evidently we are not meant to remain children always. The time comes when we must put away childish things and obey the summons of truth, stern and high. A people who fear the truth can never he a free people. If what I will say is the truth, do you know of any good reason why I should not say it? And if for prudential reasons I should sometimes hold back the truth, how would you know *when* I am telling what I believe to be the truth, and when I am holding it back for reasons of policy?

The truth, however unwelcome, is not injurious; it is error which raises false hopes, which destroys, degrades and pollutes, and which, sooner or later, must be abandoned. Was it not Spencer, whom Darwin called "our great philosopher," who said, "Repulsive as is its aspect, the hard fact which dissipates a cherished illusion is presently found to contain the germ of a more salutary belief?" Spain is decaying today because her teachers, for policy's sake, are withholding the disagreeable truth from the people. Holy water and sainted bones can give a nation illusions and dreams, but never,--strength.

A difficult subject is in the nature of a challenge to the mind. One difficult task attempted is worth a thousand commonplace efforts completed. The majority of people avoid the difficult and fear danger. But he who would progress must even court danger. Political and religious liberty were discovered through peril and struggle. The world owes its emancipation to human daring. Had Columbus feared danger, America might have slept for another thousand years.

I have a difficult subject in hand. It is also a delicate one. But I am determined not only to know, if it is possible, the whole truth about Jesus, but also to communicate that truth to others. Some people can keep their minds shut. I cannot; I must share my intellectual life with the world. If I lived a thousand years ago, I might have collapsed at the sight of the burning stake, but I feel sure I would have deserved the stake.

People say to me, sometimes, "Why do you not confine yourself to moral and religious exhortation, such as, 'Be kind, do good, love one another, etc.'?" But there is more of a moral tonic in the open and candid discussion of a subject like the one in hand, than in a multitude of platitudes. We feel our moral fiber stiffen into force and purpose under the inspiration of a peril dared for the advancement of truth.

"Tell us what you believe," is one of the requests frequently addressed to me. I never deliver a lecture in which I do not, either directly or indirectly, give full and free expression to my faith in everything that is worthy of faith. If I do not believe in dogma, it is because I believe in freedom. If I do not believe in one inspired book, it is because I believe that all truth and only truth is inspired. If I do not ask the gods to help us, it is because I believe in human help, so much more real than supernatural help. If I do not believe in standing still, it is because I believe in progress. If I am not attracted by the vision of a distant heaven, it is because I believe in human happiness, now and here. If I do not say "Lord, Lord!" to Jesus, it is because I bow my head to a greater Power than Jesus, to a more efficient Savior than he has ever been--Science!

"Oh, he tears down, but does not build up," is another criticism about my work. It is not true. No preacher or priest is more constructive. To build up their churches and maintain their creeds the priests pulled down and destroyed the magnificent civilization of Greece and Rome, plunging Europe into the dark and sterile ages which lasted over a thousand years. When Galileo waved his hands for joy because he believed he had enriched humanity with a new truth and extended the sphere of knowledge, what did the church do to him? It conspired to destroy him. It shut him up in a dungeon! Clapping truth into jail; gagging the mouth of the student-- is that building up or tearing down? When Bruno lighted a new torch to increase the light of the world, what was his reward? The stake! During all the ages that the church had the power to police the world, every time a thinker raised his head he was clubbed to death. Do you think it is kind of us--does it square with our sense of justice to call the priest constructive, and the scientists and philosophers who have helped people to their feet--helped them to self-government in politics, and to self-help in life,--destructive? Count your rights--political, religious, social, intellectual--and tell me which of them was conquered for you by the priest.

"He is irreverent," is still another hasty criticism I have heard advanced against the rationalist. I wish to tell you something. But first let us be impersonal. The epithets "irreverent," "blasphemer," "atheist," and "infidel," are flung at a man, not from pity, but from envy. Not having the courage or the industry of our neighbor who works like a busy bee in the world of men and books, searching with the sweat of his brow for the real bread of life, wetting the open page before him with his tears, pushing into the "wee" hours of the night his quest, animated by the fairest of all loves, "the love of truth",--we ease our own indolent conscience by calling him names. We pretend that it is not because we are too lazy or too selfish to work as hard or think as freely as he does, but because we do not want to be as irreverent as he is that we keep the windows of our minds shut. To excuse our own mediocrity we call the man who tries to get out of the rut a "blasphemer." And so we ask the world to praise our indifference as a great virtue, and to denounce the conscientious toil and thought of another, as "blasphemy."

IS JESUS A MYTH?

What is a myth? A myth is a fanciful explanation of a given phenomenon. Observing the sun, the moon, and the stars overhead, the primitive man wished to account for them. This was natural. The mind craves for knowledge. The child asks questions because of an inborn desire to know. Man feels ill at ease with a sense of a mental vacuum, until his questions are answered. Before the days of science, a fanciful answer was all that could be given to man's questions about the physical world. The primitive man guessed where knowledge failed him--what else could he do? A myth, then, is a guess, a story, a speculation, or a fanciful explanation of a phenomenon, in the absence of accurate information.

Many are the myths about the heavenly bodies, which, while we call them myths, because we know better, were to the ancients truths. The Sun and Moon were once brother and sister, thought the child-man; but there arose a dispute between them; the woman ran away, and the man ran after her, until they came to the end of the earth where land and sky met. The woman jumped into the sky, and the man after her, where they kept chasing each other forever, as Sun and Moon. Now and then they came close enough to snap at each other. That was their explanation of an eclipse. (Childhood of the World.--Edward Clodd.) With this mythus, the primitive man was satisfied, until his developing intelligence realized its inadequacy. Science was born of that realization.

During the middle ages it was believed by Europeans that in certain parts of the world, in India, for instance, there were people who had only one eye in the middle of their foreheads, and were more like monsters than humans. This was imaginary knowledge, which travel and research have corrected. The myth of a one-eyed people living in India has been replaced by accurate information concerning the Hindoos. Likewise, before the science of ancient languages was perfected--before archaeology had dug up buried cities and deciphered the hieroglyphics on the monuments of antiquity, most of our knowledge concerning the earlier ages was mythical, that is to say, it was knowledge not based on investigation, but made to order. Just as the theologians still speculate about the other world, primitive man speculated about this world. Even we moderns, not very long ago, believed, for instance, that the land of Egypt was visited by ten fantastic plagues; that in one bloody night every first born in the land was slain; that the angel of a tribal-god dipped his hand in blood and printed a red mark upon the doors of the houses of the Jews to protect them from harm; that Pharaoh and his armies were drowned in the Red Sea; that the children of Israel wandered for forty years around Mount Sinai; and so forth, and so forth. But now that we can read the inscriptions on the stone pages dug out of ancient ruins; now that we can compel a buried world to reveal its secret and to tell us its story, we do not have to go on making myths about the ancients. Myths die when history is born.

It will be seen from these examples that there is no harm in myth- making if the myth is called a myth. It is when we use our fanciful knowledge to deny or to shut out real and scientific knowledge that the myth becomes a stumbling block. And this is precisely the use to which myths have been put. The king with his sword and the priest with his curses, have supported the myth against science. When a man **pretends** to believe that the **Santa Claus** of his childhood is real, and tries to compel also others to play a part, he becomes positively immoral. There is no harm in believing in **Santa Claus** as a myth, but there is in pretending that he is real, because such an attitude of mind makes a mere trifle of truth.

Is Jesus a myth? There is in man a faculty for fiction. Before history was born, there was myth; before men could think, they dreamed. It was with the human race in its infancy as it is with the child. The child's imagination is more active than its reason. It is easier for it to fancy even than to see. It thinks less than it guesses. This wild flight of fancy is checked only by experience. It is reflection which introduces a bit into the mouth of imagination, curbing its pace and subduing its restless spirit. It is, then, as we grow older, and, if I may use the word, riper, that we learn to distinguish between fact and fiction, between history and myth.

In childhood we need playthings, and the more fantastic and **bizarre** they are, the better we are pleased with them. We dream, for instance, of castles in the air--gorgeous and clothed with the azure hue of the skies. We fill the space about and over us with spirits, fairies, gods, and other invisible and airy beings. We covet the rainbow. We reach out for the moon. Our feet do not really begin to touch the firm ground until we have reached the years of discretion.

I know there are those who wish they could always remain children,--living in dreamland. But even if this were desirable, it is not possible. Evolution is our destiny; of what use is it, then, to take up arms against destiny?

Let it be borne in mind that all the religions of the world were born in the childhood of the race.

Science was not born until man had matured. There is in this thought a world of meaning.

Children make religions.

Grown up people create science.

The cradle is the womb of all the fairies and faiths of mankind.

The school is the birthplace of science.

Religion is the science of the child.

Science is the religion of the matured man.

In the discussion of this subject, I appeal to the mature, not to the child mind. I appeal to those who have cultivated a taste for truth--who are not easily scared, but who can "screw their courage to the sticking point" and follow to the end truth's leading. The multitude is ever joined to its idols; let them alone. I speak to the discerning few.

There is an important difference between a lecturer and an ordained preacher. The latter can command a hearing in the name of God, or in the name of the Bible. He does not have to satisfy his hearers about the reasonableness of what he preaches. He is God's mouthpiece, and no one may disagree with him. He can also invoke the authority of the church and of the Christian world to enforce acceptance of his teaching. The only way I may command your respect is to be reasonable. You will not listen to me for God's sake, nor for the Bible's sake, nor yet for the love of heaven, or the fear of hell. My only protection is to be rational--to be truthful. In other words, the preacher can afford to ignore common sense in the name of Revelation. But if I depart from it in the least, or am caught once playing fast and loose with the facts, I will irretrievably lose my standing.

Our answer to the question, Is Jesus a Myth? must depend more or less upon original research, as there is very little written on the subject. The majority of writers assume that a person answering to the description of Jesus lived some two thousand years ago. Even the few who entertain doubts on the subject, seem to hold that while there is a large mythical element in the Jesus story, nevertheless there is a historical nucleus round which has clustered the elaborate legend of the Christ. In all probability, they argue, there was a man called Jesus, who said many helpful things, and led an exemplary life, and all the miracles and wonders represent the accretions of fond and pious ages.

Let us place ourselves entirely in the hands of the evidence. As far as possible, let us be passive, showing no predisposition one way or another. We can afford to be independent. If the evidence proves the historicity of Jesus, well and good; if the evidence is not sufficient to prove it, there is no reason why we should fear to say so; besides, it is our duty to inform ourselves on this question. As intelligent beings we desire to know whether this Jesus, whose worship is not only costing the world millions of the people's money, but which is also drawing to his service the time, the energies, the affection, the devotion, and the labor of humanity,--is a myth, or a reality. We believe that all religious persecutions, all sectarian wars, hatreds and intolerance, which still cramp and embitter our humanity, would be replaced by love and brotherhood, if the sects could be made to see that the God-Jesus they are quarreling over is a myth, a shadow to which credulity alone gives substance. Like people who have been fighting in the dark, fearing some danger, the sects, once relieved of the thraldom of a tradition which has been handed down to them by a childish age and country, will turn around and embrace one another. In every sense, the subject is an all-absorbing one. It goes to the root of things; it touches the vital parts, and it means life or death to the Christian religion.

THE PROBLEM STATED

Let me now give an idea of the method I propose to follow in the study of this subject. Let us suppose that a student living in the year 3000 desired to make sure that such a man as Abraham Lincoln really lived and did the things attributed to him. How would he go about it?

A man must have a birthplace and a birthday. All the records agree as to where and when Lincoln was born. This is not enough to prove his historicity, but it is an important link in the chain.

Neither the place nor the time of Jesus' birth is known. There has never been any unanimity about this matter. There has been considerable confusion and contradiction about it. It cannot be proved that the twenty-fifth of December is his birthday. A number of other dates were observed by the Christian church at various times as the birthday of Jesus. The Gospels give no date, and appear to be quite uncertain--really ignorant about it. When it is remembered that the Gospels purport to have been written by Jesus' intimate companions, and during the lifetime of his brothers and mother, their silence on this matter becomes significant. The selection of the twenty-fifth of December as his birthday is not only an arbitrary one, but that date, having been from time immemorial dedicated to the Sun, the inference is that the Son of God and the Sun of heaven enjoying the same birthday, were at one time identical beings. The fact that Jesus' death was accompanied with the darkening of the Sun, and that the date of his resurrection is also associated with the position of the Sun at the time of the vernal equinox, is a further intimation that we have in the story of the birth, death, and resurrection of Jesus, an ancient and nearly universal Sun-myth, instead of verifiable historical events. The story of Jesus for three days in the heart of the earth; of Jonah, three days in the belly of a fish; of Hercules, three days in the belly of a whale, and of Little Red Riding Hood, sleeping in the belly of a great black wolf, represent the attempt of primitive man to explain the phenomenon of Day and Night. The Sun is swallowed by a dragon, a wolf, or a whale, which plunges the world into darkness; but the dragon is killed, and the Sun rises triumphant to make another Day. This ancient Sun myth is the starting point of nearly all miraculous religions, from the days of Egypt to the twentieth century.

The story which Mathew relates about a remarkable star, which sailing in the air pointed out to some unnamed magicians the cradle or cave in which the wonder-child was born, helps further to identify Jesus with the Sun. What became of this "performing" star, or of the magicians, and their costly gifts, the records do not say. It is more likely that it was the astrological predilections of the gospel writer which led him to assign to his God-child a star in the heavens. The belief that the stars determine human destinies is a very ancient one. Such expressions in our language as "ill-starred," "a lucky star," "disaster," "lunacy," and so on, indicate the hold which astrology once enjoyed upon the human mind. We still call a melancholy man, *Saturnine*; a cheerful man, *Jovial*; a quick-tempered man, *Mercurial*; showing how closely our ancestors associated the movements of celestial bodies with human affairs[1]. The prominence, therefore, of the sun and stars in the Gospel story tends to show that Jesus is an astrological rather than a historical character.

That the time of his birth, his death, and supposed resurrection is ***not*** verifiable is generally admitted.

This uncertainty robs the story of Jesus, to an extent at least, of the atmosphere of reality.

The twenty-fifth of December is celebrated as his birthday. Yet there is no evidence that he was born on that day. Although the Gospels are silent as to the date on which Jesus was born, there is circumstantial evidence in the accounts given of the event to show that the twenty- fifth of December could not have been his birthday. It snows in Palestine, though a warmer country, and we know that in Decem-

---

1   Childhood of the World.--Edward Clodd.

ber there are no shepherds tending their flocks in the night time in that country. Often at this time of the year the fields and hills are covered with snow. Hence, if the shepherds sleeping in the fields really saw the heavens open and heard the angel-song, in all probability it was in some other month of the year, and not late in December. We know, also, that early in the history of Christianity the months of May and June enjoyed the honor of containing the day of Jesus' birth.

Of course, it is immaterial on which day Jesus was born, but why is it not known? Yet not only is the date of his birth a matter of conjecture, but also the year in which he was born. Matthew, one of the Evangelists, suggests that Jesus was born in King Herod's time, for it was this king who, hearing from the Magi that a King of the Jews was born, decided to destroy him; but Luke, another Evangelist, intimates that Jesus was born when Quirinus was ruler of Judea, which makes the date of Jesus' birth about fourteen years later than the date given by Matthew. Why this discrepancy in a historical document, to say nothing about inspiration? The theologian might say that this little difficulty was introduced purposely into the scriptures to establish its infallibility, but it is only religious books that are pronounced infallible on the strength of the contradictions they contain.

Again, Matthew says that to escape the evil designs of Herod, Mary and Joseph, with the infant Jesus, fled into Egypt, Luke says nothing about this hurried flight, nor of Herod's intention to kill the infant Messiah. On the contrary he tells us that after the forty days of purification were over Jesus was publicly presented at the temple, where Herod, if he really, as Matthew relates, wished to seize him, could have done so without difficulty. It is impossible to reconcile the flight to Egypt with the presentation in the temple, and this inconsistency is certainly insurmountable and makes it look as if the narrative had no value whatever as history.

When we come to the more important chapters about Jesus, we meet with greater difficulties. Have you ever noticed that the day on which Jesus is supposed to have died falls invariably on a Friday? What is the reason for this? It is evident that nobody knows, and nobody ever knew the date on which the Crucifixion took place, if it ever took place. It is so obscure and so mythical that an artificial day has been fixed by the Ecclesiastical councils. While it is always on a Friday that the Crucifixion is commemorated, the week in which the day occurs varies from year to year. "Good Friday" falls not before the spring equinox, but as soon after the spring equinox as the full moon allows, thus making the calculation to depend upon the position of the sun in the Zodiac and the phases of the moon. But that was precisely the way the day for the festival of the pagan goddess Oestera was determined. The Pagan Oestera has become the Christian Easter. Does not this fact, as well as those already touched upon, make the story of Jesus to read very much like the stories of the Pagan deities.

The early Christians, Origin, for instance, in his reply to the rationalist Celsus who questioned the reality of Jesus, instead of producing evidence of a historical nature, appealed to the mythology of the pagans to prove that the story of Jesus was no more incredible than those of the Greek and Roman gods. This is so important that we refer our readers to Origin's own words on the subject. "Before replying to Celsus, it is necessary to admit that in the matter of history, however true it might be," writes this Christian Father, "it is often very difficult and sometimes quite impossible to establish its truth by evidence which shall be considered sufficient."[2] This is a plain admission that as early as the second and third centuries the claims put forth about Jesus did not admit of positive historical demonstration. But in the absence of evidence Origin offers the following metaphysical arguments against the sceptical Celsus: 1. Such stories as are told of Jesus are admitted to be true when told of pagan divinities, why can they not also be true when told of the Christian Messiah? 2. They must be true because they are the fulfillment of Old Testament prophecies. In other words, the only proofs Origin can bring forth against the rationalistic criticism of Celsus is, that to deny Jesus would be equivalent to denying both the Pagan and Jewish mythologies. If Jesus is not real, says Origin, then Apollo was not real, and the Old Testament prophecies have not been fulfilled. If we are to have any mythology at all, he seems to argue, why object to adding to it the mythus of Jesus? There could not be a more damaging admission than this from one of the most conspicuous defenders of Jesus' story against early criticism.

Justin Martyr, another early Father, offers the following argument against unbelievers in the Christian legend: "When we say also that the Word, which is the first birth of God, was produced without sexual union, and that he, Jesus Christ, our teacher, was crucified, died, and rose again, and ascended into heaven, we propound nothing different from what you believe regarding those whom you esteem sons of

---

2 Origin *Contre Celse.* 1. 58 et Suiv. Ibid.

Jupiter."[3] Which is another way of saying that the Christian mythus is very similar to the pagan, and should therefore be equally true. Pressing his argument further, this interesting Father discovers many resemblances between what he himself is preaching and what the pagans have always believed: "For you know how many sons your esteemed writers ascribe to Jupiter. Mercury, the interpreting word (he spells this word with a small *w* while in the above quotation he uses a capital *w* to denote the Christian incarnation) and teacher of all; Aesculapius...who ascended to heaven; one Hercules...and Perseus;...and Bellerophon, who, though sprung from mortals, rose to heaven on the horses of Pegasus." [Note: Ibid.] If Jupiter can have, Justin Martyr seems to reason, half a dozen divine sons, why cannot Jehovah have at least one?

Instead of producing historical evidence or appealing to creditable documents, as one would to prove the existence of a Caesar or an Alexander, Justin Martyr draws upon pagan mythology in his reply to the critics of Christianity. All he seems to ask for is that Jesus be given a higher place among the divinities of the ancient world.

To help their cause the Christian apologists not infrequently also changed the sense of certain Old Testament passages to make them support the miraculous stories in the New Testament. For example, having borrowed from Oriental books the story of the god in a manger, surrounded by staring animals, the Christian fathers introduced a prediction of this event into the following text from the book of Habakkuk in the Bible: "Accomplish thy work in the midst of the *years*, in the midst of the years make known, etc." [Note: Hab. iii. 2.] This Old Testament text appeared in the Greek translation as follows: "Thou shalt manifest thyself in the midst of *two animals*" which was fulfilled of course when Jesus was born in a stable. How weak must be one's case to resort to such tactics in order to command a following! And when it is remembered that these follies were deemed necessary to prove the reality of what has been claimed as the most stupendous event in all history, one can readily see upon how fragile a foundation is built the story of the Christian God-man.

Let us continue: Abraham Lincoln's associates and contemporaries are all known to history. The immediate companions of Jesus appear to be, on the other hand, as mythical as he is himself. Who was Matthew? Who was Mark? Who were

---

3   First Apology, Chapter xxi (Anti-Nicene Library).

John, Peter, Judas, and Mary? There is absolutely no evidence that they ever existed. They are not mentioned except in the New Testament books, which, as we shall see, are "supposed" copies of "supposed" originals. If Peter ever went to Rome with a new doctrine, how is it that no historian has taken note of him? If Paul visited Athens and preached from Mars Hill, how is it that there is no mention of him or of his strange Gospel in the Athenian chronicles? For all we know, both Peter and Paul may have really existed, but it is only a guess, as we have no means of ascertaining. The uncertainty about the apostles of Jesus is quite in keeping with the uncertainty about Jesus himself.

The report that Jesus had twelve apostles seems also mythical. The number twelve, like the number seven, or three, or forty, plays an important role in all Sun-myths, and points to the twelve signs of the Zodiac. Jacob had twelve sons; there were twelve tribes of Israel; twelve months in the year; twelve gates or pillars of heaven, etc. In many of the religions of the world, the number twelve is sacred. There have been few god-saviors who did not have twelve apostles or messengers. In one or two places, in the New Testament, Jesus is made to send out "the seventy" to evangelize the world. Here again we see the presence of a myth. It was believed that there were seventy different nations in the world--to each nation an apostle. Seventy wise men are supposed to have translated the Old Testament, sitting in seventy different cells. That is why their translation is called "*the Septuagint*" But it is all a legend, as there is no evidence of seventy scholars working in seventy individual cells on the Hebrew Bible. One of the Church Fathers declares that he saw these seventy cells with his own eyes. He was the only one who saw them.

That the "Twelve Apostles" are fanciful may he inferred from the obscurity in which the greater number of them have remained. Peter, Paul, John, James, Judas, occupy the stage almost exclusively. If Paul was an apostle, we have fourteen, instead of twelve. Leaving out Judas, and counting Matthias, who was elected in his place, we have thirteen apostles.

The number forty figures also in many primitive myths. The Jews were in the wilderness for forty years; Jesus fasted for forty days; from the resurrection to the ascension were forty days; Moses was on the mountain with God for forty days. An account in which such scrupulous attention is shown to supposed sacred numbers is apt to be more artificial than real. The biographers of Lincoln or of Socrates do not seem to be interested in numbers. They write history, not stories.

Again, many of the contemporaries of Lincoln bear written witness to his existence. The historians of the time, the statesmen, the publicists, the chroniclers--all seem to be acquainted with him, or to have heard of him. It is impossible to explain why the contemporaries of Jesus, the authors and historians of his time, do not take notice of him. If Abraham Lincoln was important enough to have attracted the attention of his contemporaries, how much more Jesus. Is it reasonable to suppose that these Pagan and Jewish writers knew of Jesus,--had heard of his incomparably great works and sayings,--but omitted to give him a page or a line? Could they have been in a conspiracy against him? How else is this unanimous silence to be accounted for? Is it not more likely that the wonder-working Jesus was unknown to them? And he was unknown to them because no such Jesus existed in their day.

Should the student, looking into Abraham Lincoln's history, discover that no one of his biographers knew positively just when he lived or where he was born, he would have reason to conclude that because of this uncertainty on the part of the biographers, he must be more exacting than he otherwise would have been. That is precisely our position. Of course, there are in history great men of whose birthplaces or birthdays we are equally uncertain. But we believe in their existence, not because no one seems to know exactly when and where they were born, but because there is overwhelming evidence corroborating the other reports about them, and which is sufficient to remove the suspicion suggested by the darkness hanging over their nativity. Is there any evidence strong enough to prove the historicity of Jesus, in spite of the fact that not even his supposed companions, writing during the lifetime of Jesus' mother, have any definite information to give.

But let us continue. The reports current about a man like Lincoln are verifiable, while many of those about Jesus are of a nature that no amount of evidence can confirm. That Lincoln was President of these United States, that he signed the Emancipation Proclamation, and that he was assassinated, can be readily authenticated.

But how can any amount of evidence satisfy one's self that Jesus was born of a virgin, for instance? Such a report or rumor can never even be examined; it does not lend itself to evidence; it is beyond the sphere of history; it is not a legitimate question for investigation. It belongs to mythology. Indeed, to put forth a report of that nature is to forbid the use of evidence, and to command forcible acquiescence, which, to say the least, is a very suspicious circumstance, calculated to hurt rather than to help the Jesus story.

The report that Jesus was God is equally impossible of verification. How are we to prove whether or not a certain person was God? Jesus may have been a wonderful man, but is every wonderful man a God? Jesus may have claimed to have been a God, but is every one who puts forth such a claim a God? How, then, are we to decide which of the numerous candidates for divine honors should be given our votes? And can we by voting for Jesus make him a God? Observe to what confusion the mere attempt to follow such a report leads us.

A human Jesus may or may not have existed, but we are as sure as we can be of anything, that a virgin-born God, named Jesus, such as we must believe in or be eternally lost, is an impossibility--except to credulity. But credulity is no evidence at all, even when it is dignified by the name of *faith*. Let us pause for a moment to reflect: The final argument for the existence of the miraculous Jesus, preached in church and Sunday-school, these two thousand years, as the sole savior of the world, is an appeal to faith--the same to which Mohammed resorts to establish his claims, and Brigham Young to prove his revelation. There is no other possible way by which the virgin- birth or the *godhood* of a man can be established. And such a faith is never free, it is always maintained by the sword now, and by hell-fire hereafter.

Once more, if it had been reported of Abraham Lincoln that he predicted his own assassination; that he promised some of his friends they would not die until they saw him coming again upon the clouds of heaven; that he would give them thrones to sit upon; that they could safely drink deadly poisons in his name, or that he would grant them any request which they might make, provided they asked it for his sake, we would be justified in concluding that such a Lincoln never existed. Yet the most impossible utterances are put in Jesus' mouth. He is made to say: "Whatsoever ye shall ask in my name that will I do." No man who makes such a promise can keep it. It is not sayings like the above that can prove a man a God. Has Jesus kept his promise? Does he give his people everything, or "whatsoever" they ask of him? But, it is answered, "Jesus only meant to say that he would give whatever he himself considered good for his friends to have." Indeed! Is that the way to crawl out of a contract? If that is what he meant, why did he say something else? Could he not have *said* just what he *meant*, in the first place? Would it not have been fairer not to have given his friends any occasion for false expectations? Better to promise a little and do more, than to promise everything and do nothing. But to say that Jesus really entered into any such agreement is to throw doubt upon his existence. Such a character is too wild to be real. Only a mythical Jesus could virtually hand over the government of the universe to courtiers who have petitions to press upon his attention. Moreover, if Jesus could keep his promise, there would be today no misery in the world, no orphans, no childless mothers, no shipwrecks, no floods, no famines, no disease, no crippled children, no insanity, no wars, no crime, no wrong! Have not a thousand, thousand prayers been offered in Jesus' name against every evil which has ploughed the face of our earth? Have these prayers been answered? Then why is there discontent in the world? Can the followers of Jesus move mountains, drink deadly poisons, touch serpents, or work greater miracles than are ascribed to Jesus, as it was promised that they would do? How many self-deluded prophets these extravagant claims have produced! And who can number the bitter disappointments caused by such impossible promises?

George Jacob Holyoake, of England, tells how in the days of utter poverty, his believing mother asked the Lord, again and again--on her knees, with tears streaming from her eyes, and with absolute faith in Jesus' ability to keep His promise,--to give her starving children their daily bread. But the more fervently she prayed the heavier grew the burden of her life. A stone or wooden idol could not have been more indifferent to a mother's tears. "My mind aches as I think of those days," writes Mr. Holyoake. One day he went to see the Rev. Mr. Cribbace, who had invited inquirers to his house. "Do you really believe," asked young Holyoake to the clergyman, "that what we ask in faith we shall receive?" "It never struck me," continues Mr. Holyoake, "that the preacher's threadbare dress, his half-famished look, and necessity of taking up a collection the previous night to pay expenses showed that faith was not a source of income to him. It never struck me that if help could be obtained by prayer no church would be needy, no believer would be poor." What answer did the preacher give to Holyoake's earnest question? The same which the preachers of today give: "He parried his answer with many words, and at length said that the promise was to be taken with the provision that what we asked for would be given, *if God thought it for our good.*" Why then, did not Jesus explain that important ***proviso*** when he made the promise? Was Jesus only making a half statement, the other half of which he would reveal later to protect himself against disappointed petitioners. But he said: "If ye ask anything in my name, I will do it," and "If it were not so, I would have told you." Did he not mean just what he said? The truth is that no historical person in his senses ever made such extraordinary, such impossible promises, and the report that Jesus made them only goes to confirm that their author is only a legendary being.

When this truth dawned upon Mr. Holyoake he ceased to petition Heaven, which was like "dropping a bucket into an empty well," and began to look ***elsewhere*** for help. [Note: Bygones Worth Remembering.--George Jacob Holyoake] The world owes its advancement to the fact that men no longer look to Heaven for help, but help themselves. Self-effort, and not prayer, is the remedy against ignorance, slavery, poverty, and moral degradation. Fortunately, by holding up before us an impossible Jesus, with his impossible promises, the churches have succeeded only in postponing, but not in preventing, the progress of man. This is a compliment to human nature, and it is well earned. It is also a promise that in time humanity will be completely emancipated from every phantom which in the past has scared it into silence or submission, and

> "A loftier race than e'er the world
> Hath known shall rise
>   With flame of liberty in their souls,
>   And light of science in their eyes."

THE CHRISTIAN DOCUMENTS

The documents containing the story of Jesus are so unlike those about Lincoln or any other historical character, that we must be doubly vigilant in our investigation.

The Christians rely mainly on the four Gospels for the historicity of Jesus. But the original documents of which the books in the New Testament are claimed to be faithful copies are not in existence. ***There is absolutely no evidence that they ever were in existence***. This is a statement which can not be controverted. Is it conceivable that the early believers lost through carelessness or purposely ***every*** document written by an apostle, while guarding with all protecting jealousy and zeal the writings of anonymous persons? Is there any valid reason why the contributions to Christian literature of an inspired apostle should perish while those of a nameless scribe are preserved, why the original Gospel of Matthew should drop quietly out of sight, no one knows how, while a supposed copy of it in an alien language is preserved for many centuries? Jesus himself, it is admitted, did not write a single line. He had come, according to popular belief, to reveal the will of God--a most important mission indeed, and yet he not only did not put this revelation in writing during his lifetime, and with his own hand, which it is natural to suppose that a divine teacher, expressly come from heaven, would have done, but he left this all-important duty to anonymous chroniclers, who, naturally, made enough mistakes to split up Christendom into innumerable factions. It is worth a moment's pause to think of the persecutions, the cruel wars, and the centuries of hatred and bitterness which would have been spared our unfortunate humanity, if Jesus himself had written down his message in the clearest and plainest manner, instead of leaving it to his supposed disciples to publish it to the world, when he could no longer correct their mistakes.

Moreover, not only did Jesus not write himself, but he has not even taken any pains to preserve the writings of his "apostles," It is well known that the original manuscripts, if there were any, are nowhere to be found. This is a grave matter. We have only supposed copies of supposed original manuscripts. Who copied them? When were they copied? How can we be sure that these copies are reliable? And why are there thousands upon thousands of various readings in these, numerous supposed copies? What means have we of deciding which version or reading to accept? Is it possible that as the result of Jesus' advent into our world, we have only a basketful of nameless and dateless copies and documents? Is it conceivable, I ask, that a God would send his Son to us, and then leave us to wander through a pile of dusty manuscripts to find out why He sent His Son, and what He taught when on earth?

The only answer the Christian church can give to this question is that the original writings were purposely allowed to perish. When a precious document containing the testament of Almighty God, and inscribed for an eternal purpose by the Holy Ghost, disappears altogether there is absolutely no other way of accounting for its disappearance than by saying, as we have suggested, that its divine author must have intentionally withdrawn it from circulation. "God moves in a mysterious way" is the last resort of the believer. This is the one argument which is left to theology to fight science with. Unfortunately it is an argument which would prove every cult and "ism" under the heavens true. The Mohammedan, the Mazdaian, and the Pagan may also fall back upon faith. There is nothing which faith can not cover up from the light. But if a faith which ignores evidence be not a superstition, what then is superstition? I wonder if the Catholic Church, which pretends to believe--and which derives quite an income from the belief--that God has miraculously preserved the wood of the cross, the Holy Sepulchre, in Jerusalem, the coat of Jesus, and quite a number of other mementos, can explain why the original manuscripts were lost. I have a suspicion that there were no "original" manuscripts. I am not sure of this, of course, but if nails, bones and holy places could be miraculously preserved, why not also manuscripts? It is reasonable to suppose that the Deity would not have permitted the most important documents containing His Revelation to drop into some hole and disappear, or to be gnawed into dust by the insects, after having had them written by special inspiration.

Again, when these documents, such as we find them, are examined, it will be observed that, even in the most elementary intelligence which they pretend to furnish, they are hopelessly at variance with one another. It is, for example, utterly impossible to reconcile Matthew's genealogy of Jesus with the one given by Luke. In copying the names of the supposed ancestors of Jesus, they tamper with the list as given in the book of Chronicles, in the Old Testament, and thereby justly expose themselves to the charge of bad faith. One evangelist says Jesus was descended from Solomon, born of "her that had been the wife of Urias." It will be remembered that David ordered Urias killed in a cowardly manner, that he may marry his widow, whom he coveted. According to Matthew, Jesus is one of the offspring of this adulterous relation. According to Luke, it is not through Solomon, but through Nathan, that Jesus is connected with the house of David.

Again, Luke tells us that the name of the father of Joseph was *Heli;* Matthew says it was ***Jacob***. If the writers of the gospels were contemporaries of Joseph they could have easily learned the exact name of his father.

Again, why do these biographers of Jesus give us the genealogy of Joseph if he was not the father of Jesus? It is the genealogy of Mary which they should have given to prove the descent of Jesus from the house of David, and not that of Joseph. These irreconcilable differences between Luke, Matthew and the other evangelists, go to prove that these authors possessed no reliable information concerning the subjects they were writing about. For if Jesus is a historical character, and these biographers were really his immediate associates, and were inspired besides, how are we to explain their blunders and contradictions about his genealogy?

A good illustration of the mythical or unhistorical character of the New Testament is furnished by the story of John the Baptist. He is first represented as confessing publicly that Jesus is the Christ; that he himself is not worthy to unloose the latchet of his shoes; and that Jesus is the Lamb of God, "who taketh away the sins of the world." John was also present, the gospels say, when the heavens opened and a dove descended on Jesus' head, and he heard the voice from the skies, crying: "He is my beloved Son, in whom I am well pleased."

Is it possible that, a few chapters later, this same John forgets his public confession,--the dove and the voice from heaven,--and actually sends two of his disciples to find out who this Jesus is, [Note: Matthew xi.] The only way we can account for such strange conduct is that the compiler or editor in question had two different myths or stories before him, and he wished to use them both.

A further proof of the loose and extravagant style of the Gospel writers is furnished by the concluding verse of the Fourth Gospel: "There are also many other things which Jesus did, the which, if they should be written, every one, I suppose that even the world itself could not contain the books that should be written." This is more like the language of a myth-maker than of a historian. How much reliance can we put in a reporter who is given to such exaggeration? To say that the world itself would be too small to contain the unreported sayings and doings of a teacher whose public life possibly did not last longer than a year, and whose reported words and deeds fill only a few pages, is to prove one's statements unworthy of serious consideration.

And it is worth our while to note also that the documents which have come down to our time and which purport to be the biographies of Jesus, are not only written in an alien language, that is to say, in a language which was not that of Jesus and his disciples, but neither are they dated or signed. Jesus and his twelve apostles were Jews; why are all the four Gospels written in Greek? If they were originally written in Hebrew, how can we tell that the Greek translation is accurate, since we can not compare it with the originals? And why are these Gospels anonymous? Why are they not dated? But as we shall say something more on this subject in the present volume, we confine ourselves at this point to reproducing a fragment of the manuscript pages from which our Greek Translations have been made.[Note: See page 57.] It is admitted by scholars that owing to the difficulty of reading these ancient and imperfect and also conflicting texts, an accurate translation is impossible. But this is another way of saying that what the churches call the Word of God is not only the word of man, but a very imperfect word, at that.

The belief in Jesus, then, is founded on secondary documents, altered and edited by various hands; on lost originals, and on anonymous manuscripts of an age considerably later than the events therein related--manuscripts which contradict each other as well as themselves. Such is clearly and undeniably the basis for the belief in a historical Jesus. It was this sense of the insufficiency of the evidence which drove the missionaries of Christianity to commit forgeries.

If there was ample evidence for the historicity of Jesus, why did his biographers resort to forgery? The following admissions by Christian writers themselves show the helplessness of the early preachers in the presence of inquirers who asked for proofs. The church historian, Mosheim, writes that, "The Christian Fathers deemed it a pious act to employ deception and fraud." [Note: Ecclesiastical Hist., Vol. I, P. 247.]

Again, he says: "The greatest and most pious teachers were nearly all of them infected with this leprosy." Will not some believer tell us why forgery and fraud were necessary to prove the historicity of Jesus. Another historian, Milman, writes that, "Pious fraud was admitted and avowed" by the early missionaries of Jesus. "It was an age of literary frauds," writes Bishop Ellicott, speaking of the times immediately following the alleged crucifixion of Jesus. Dr. Giles declares that, "There can be no doubt that great numbers of books were written with no other purpose than to deceive." And it is the opinion of Dr. Robertson Smith that, "There was an enormous floating mass of spurious literature created to suit party views." Books which are now rejected as apochryphal were at one time received as inspired, and books which are now believed to be infallible were at one time regarded as of no authority in the Christian world. It certainly is puzzling that there should be a whole literature of fraud and forgery in the name of a historical person. But if Jesus was a myth, we can easily explain the legends and traditions springing up in his name.

The early followers of Jesus, then, realizing the force of this objection, did actually resort to interpolation and forgery in order to prove that Jesus was a historical character.

One of the oldest critics of the Christian religion was a Pagan, known to history under the name of Porphyry; yet, the early Fathers did not hesitate to tamper even with the writings of an avowed opponent of their religion. After issuing an edict to destroy, among others, the writings of this philosopher, a work, called ***Philosophy of Oracles,*** was produced, in which the author is made to write almost as a Christian; and the name of Porphyry was signed to it as its author. St. Augustine was one of the first to reject it as a forgery. [Note: Geo. W. Foote. Crimes of Christianity.] A more astounding invention than this alleged work of a heathen bearing witness to Christ is difficult to produce. Do these forgeries, these apocryphal writings, these interpolations, freely admitted to have been the prevailing practice of the early Christians, help to prove the existence of Jesus? And when to this wholesale manufacture of doubtful evidence is added the terrible vandalism which nearly destroyed every great Pagan classic, we can form an idea of the desperate means to which the early Christians resorted to prove that Jesus was not a myth. It all goes to show how difficult it is to make a man out of a myth.

VIRGIN BIRTHS

Stories of gods born of virgins are to be found in nearly every age and country. There have been many virgin mothers, and Mary with her child is but a recent version of a very old and universal myth. In China and India, in Babylonia and Egypt, in Greece and Rome, "divine" beings selected from among the daughters of men the purest and most beautiful to serve them as a means of entrance into the world of mortals. Wishing to take upon themselves the human form, while retaining at the same time their "divinity," this compromise--of an earthly mother with a "divine" father--was effected. In the form of a swan Jupiter approached Leda, as in the guise of a dove, or a ***Paracletus,*** Jehovah "overshadowed" Mary.

A nymph bathing in a river in China is touched by a lotus plant, and the divine Fohi is born.

In Siam, a wandering sunbeam caresses a girl in her teens, and the great and wonderful deliverer, Codom, is born. In the life of Buddha we read that he descended on his mother Maya, "in likeness as the heavenly queen, and entered her womb," and was "born from her right side, to save the world." [Note: Stories of Virgin Births. Reference: Lord Macartney. Voyage dans 'interview de la Chine et en Tartarie. Vol. I, P. 48. See also Les Vierges Meres et les Naissance Miraculeuse. P. Saintyves. P. 19, etc.] In Greece, the young god Apollo visits a fair maid of Athens, and a Plato is ushered into the world.

In ancient Mexico, as well as in Babylonia, and in modern Corea, as in modern Palestine, as in the legends of all lands, virgins gave birth and became divine mothers. [Note: Stories of Virgin Births. Reference: Lord Macartney. Voyage dans 'interview de la Chine et en Tartarie. Vol. I, P. 48. See also Les Vierges Meres et les Naissance Miraculeuse. P. Saintyves. P. 19, etc.]

But the real home of virgin births is the land of the Nile. Eighteen hundred years before Christ, we find carved on one of the walls of the great temple of Luxor a picture of the ***annunciation, conception and birth*** of King Amunothph III, an almost exact copy of the annunciation, conception and birth of the Christian God. Of course no one will think of maintaining that the Egyptians borrowed the idea from the Catholics nearly two thousand years before the Christian era. "The story in the Gospel of Luke, the first and second chapters is, "says Malvert, "a reproduction, 'point by point,' of the story in stone of the miraculous birth of Amunothph." [Note: Science and Religion P. 96.]

Sharpe in his Egyptian Mythology, page 19, gives the following description of the Luxor picture, quoted by G. W. Foote in his ***Bible Romances,*** page 126: "In this picture we have the annunciation, the conception, the birth and the adoration, as described in the first and second chapters of Luke's Gospel." Massey gives a more minute description of the Luxor picture. "The first scene on the left hand shows the god Taht, the divine Word or Loges, in the act of hailing the virgin queen, announcing to her that she is to give birth to a son. In the second scene the god Kneph (assisted by Hathor) gives life to her. This is the Holy Ghost, or Spirit that causes conception....Next the mother is seated on the midwife's stool, and the child is supported in the hands of one of the nurses. The fourth scene is that of the adoration. Here the child is enthroned, receiving homage from the gods and gifts from men." [Note: Natural Genesis. Massey, Vol. II, P. 398.] The picture on the wall of the Luxor temple, then, is one of the sources to which the anonymous writers of the Gospels went for their miraculous story. It is no wonder they suppressed their own identity as well as the source from which they borrowed their material.

Not only the idea of a virgin mother, but all the other miraculous events, such as the stable cradle, the guiding star, the massacre of the children, the flight to Egypt, and the resurrection and bodily ascension toward the clouds, have not only been borrowed, but are even scarcely altered in the New Testament story of Jesus.

That the early Christians borrowed the legend of Jesus from earthly sources is too evident to be even questioned. Gerald Massey in his great work on Egyptian origins demonstrates the identity of Mary, the mother of Jesus, with Isis, the mother of Horus. He says: "The most ancient, gold-bedizened, smoke-stained Byzantine pictures of the virgin and child represent the mythical mother as Isis, and not as a human mother of Nazareth." [Note: Vol. ii, P. 487.] Science and research have made this fact so certain that, on the one hand ignorance, and on the other, interest only, can continue to claim inspiration for the authors of the undated and unsigned fragmentary documents which pass for the Word of God. If, then, Jesus is stripped of all the borrowed legends and miracles of which he is the subject; and if we also take away from him all the teachings which collected from Jewish and Pagan sources have been attributed to him--what will be left of him? That the ideas put in his mouth have been culled and compiled from other sources is as demonstrable as the Pagan origin of the legends related of him.

Nearly every one of the dogmas and ceremonies in the Christian cult were borrowed from other and older religions. The resurrection myth, the ascension, the eucharisty, baptism, worship by kneeling or prostration, the folding of the hands on the breast, the ringing of bells and the burning of incense, the vestments and vessels used in church, the candles, "holy" water,--even the word *Mass* were all adopted and adapted by the Christians from the religions of the ancients. The Trinity is as much Pagan, as much Indian or Buddhist, as it is Christian. The idea of a Son of God is as old as the oldest cult. The sun is the son of heaven in all primitive faiths. The physical sun becomes in the course of evolution, the Son of Righteousness, or the Son of God, and heaven is personified as the Father on High. The halo around the head of Jesus, the horns of the older deities, the rays of light radiating from the heads of Hindu and Pagan gods are incontrovertible evidence that all gods were at one time--the sun in heaven.

THE ORIGIN OF THE CROSS

Only the uninformed, of whom, we regret to say, there are a great many, and who are the main support of the old religions, still believe that the cross originated with Christianity. Like the dogmas of the Trinity, the virgin birth, and the resurrection, the sign of the cross or the cross as an emblem or a symbol was borrowed from the more ancient faiths of Asia. Perhaps one of the most important discoveries which primitive man felt obliged never to be ungrateful enough to forget, was the production of fire by the friction of two sticks placed across each other in the form of a cross. As early as the stone age we find the cross carved on monuments which have been dug out of the earth and which can be seen in the museums of Europe. On the coins of later generations as well as on the altars of prehistoric times we find the "sacred" symbol of the cross. The dead in ancient cemeteries slept under the cross as they do in our day in Catholic churchyards.

In ancient Egypt, as in modern China, India, Corea, the cross is venerated by the masses as a charm of great power. In the Musee Guimet, in Paris, we have seen specimens of pre-Christian crosses. In the Louvre Museum one of the "heathen" gods carries a cross on his head. During his second journey to New Zealand, Cook was surprised to find the natives marking the graves of their dead with the cross. We saw, in the Museum of St. Germain, an ancient divinity of Gaul, before the conquest of the country by Julius Caesar, wearing a garment on which was woven a cross. In the same museum an ancient altar of Gaul under Paganism, had a cross carved upon it. That the cross was not adopted by the followers of Jesus until a later date may be inferred from the silence of the earlier gospels, Matthew, Mark and Luke, on the details of the crucifixion, which is more fully developed in the later gospel of John. The first three evangelists say nothing about the nails or the blood, and give the impression that he was hanged. Writing of the two thieves who were sentenced to receive the same punishment, Luke says, "One of the malefactors that was **hanged** with him." The idea of a bleeding Christ, such as we see on crosses in Catholic churches, is not present in these earlier descriptions of the crucifixion; the Christians of the time of Origin were called "the followers of the god who was hanged." In the fourth gospel we see the beginnings of the legend of the cross, of Jesus carrying or falling under the weight of the cross, of the nail prints in his hands and feet, of the spear drawing the blood from his side and smearing his body. Of all this, the first three evangelists are quite ignorant.

Let it be further noted that it was not until eight hundred years after the supposed crucifixion that Jesus is seen in the form of a human being on the cross. Not in any of the paintings on the ancient catacombs is found a crucified Christ. The earliest cross bearing a human being is of the eighth century. For a long time a lamb with a cross, or on a cross, was the Christian symbol, and it is a lamb which we see entombed in the "holy sepulchre." In more than one mosaic of early Christian times, it is not Jesus, but a lamb, which is bleeding for the salvation of the world. How a lamb came to play so important a role in Christianity is variously explained. The similarity between the name of the Hindu god, **Agni** and the meaning of the same word in Latin, which is a lamb, is one theory. Another is that a ram, one of the signs of the zodiac, often confounded by the ancients with a lamb, is the origin of the popular reverence for the lamb as a symbol--a reverence which all religions based on sun-worship shared. The lamb in Christianity takes away the sins of the people, just as the paschal lamb did in the Old Testament, and earlier still, just as it did in Babylonia.

To the same effect is the following letter of the bishop of Mende, in France, bearing date of the year 800 A. D.: "Because the darkness has disappeared, and because also Christ is a real man, Pope Adrian commands us to paint him under the form of a man. The lamb of God must not any longer be painted on a cross, but after a human form has been placed on the cross, there is no objection to have a lamb also represented with it, either at the foot of the cross or on the opposite side." [Note:

Translated from the French of Didron. Quoted by Malvert.] We leave it to our readers to draw the necessary conclusions from the above letter. How did a lamb hold its place on the cross for eight hundred years? If Jesus was really crucified, and that fact was a matter of history, why did it take eight hundred years for a Christian bishop to write, "now that Christ is a real man," etc.? Today, it would be considered a blasphemy to place a lamb on a cross.

On the tombstones of Christians of the fourth century are pictures representing, not Jesus, but a lamb, working the miracles mentioned in the gospels, such as multiplying the loaves and fishes, and raising Lazarus from the dead.

While the figure on the modern cross is almost naked, those on the earlier ones are clothed and completely covered. Wearing a flowing tunic, Jesus is standing straight against the cross with his arms outstretched, as though in the act of delivering an address. Frequently, at his feet, on the cross, there is still painted the figure of a lamb, which by and by, he is going to replace altogether. Gradually the robe disappears from the crucified one, until we see him crucified, as in the adjoining picture, with hardly any clothes on, and wearing an expression of great agony.

THE SILENCE OF PROFANE WRITERS

In all historical matters, we cannot ask for more than a *reasonable* assurance concerning any question. In fact, absolute certainty in any branch of human knowledge, with the exception of mathematics, perhaps, is impossible. We are finite beings, limited in all our powers, and, hence, our conclusions are not only relative, but they should ever be held subject to correction. When our law courts send a man to the gallows, they can have no more than a reasonable assurance that he is guilty; when they acquit him, they can have no more than a reasonable assurance that he is innocent. Positive assurance is unattainable. The dogmatist is the only one who claims to possess absolute certainty. But his claim is no more than a groundless assumption. When, therefore, we learn that Josephus, for instance, who lived in the same country and about the same time as Jesus, and wrote an extensive history of the men and events of his day and country, does not mention Jesus, except by interpolation, which even a Christian clergyman, Bishop Warburton, calls "a rank forgery, and a very stupid one, too," we can be reasonably sure that no such Jesus as is described in the New Testament, lived about the same time and in the same country with Josephus.

The failure of such a historian as Josephus to mention Jesus tends to make the existence of Jesus at least reasonably doubtful.

Few Christians now place any reliance upon the evidence from Josephus. The early Fathers made this Jew admit that Jesus was the Son of God. Of course, the admission was a forgery. De Quincey says the passage is known to be "a forgery by all men not lunatics." Of one other supposed reference in Josephus, Canon Farrar says: "This passage was early tampered with by the Christians." The same writer says this of a third passage: "Respecting the third passage in Josephus, the only question is whether it be partly or entirely spurious." Lardner, the great English theologian, was the first man to prove that Josephus was a poor witness for Christ.

In examining the evidence from profane writers we must remember that the silence of one contemporary author is more important than the supposed testimony of another. There was living in the same time with Jesus a great Jewish scholar by the name of Philo. He was an Alexandrian Jew, and he visited Jerusalem while Jesus was teaching and working miracles in the holy city. Yet Philo in all his works never once mentions Jesus. He does not seem to have heard of him. He could not have helped mentioning him if he had really seen him or heard of him. In one place in his works Philo is describing the difference between two Jewish names, Hosea and Jesus. Jesus, he says, means saviour of the people. What a fine opportunity for him to have added that, at that very time, there was living in Jerusalem a saviour by the name of Jesus, or one supposed to be, or claiming to be, a saviour. He could not have helped mentioning Jesus if he had ever seen or heard of him.

We have elsewhere referred to the significant silence of the Pagan historians and miscellaneous writers on the wonderful events narrated in the New Testament. But a few remarks may be added here in explanation of the supposed testimony of Tacitus.

The quotation from Tacitus is an important one. That part of the passage which concerns us is something like this:--"They have their denomination from *Chrestus,* put to death as a criminal by Pontius Pilate during the reign of Tiberius." I wish to say in the first place that this passage is not in the *History* of Tacitus, known to the ancients, but in his *Annals,* which is not quoted by any ancient writer. The *Annals* of Tacitus were not known to be in existence until the year 1468. An English writer, Mr. Ross, has undertaken, in an interesting volume, to show that the *Annals* were forged by an Italian, Bracciolini. I am not competent to say whether or not Mr. Ross proves his point. But is it conceivable that the early Christians would have ignored so valuable a testimony had they known of its existence, and would they not have known of it had it really existed? The Christian Fathers, who not only collected assiduously all that they could use to establish the reality of Jesus--but who did not hesitate even to forge passages, to invent documents, and also to destroy the testimony of witnesses unfavorable to their cause--would have certainly used the Tacitus passage had it been in existence in their day. *Not one of the Christian Fathers* in his controversy with the unbelievers has quoted the passage from Tacitus, which passage is the church's strongest proof of the historicity of Jesus, outside the gospels.

But, to begin with, this passage has the appearance, at least, of being penned by a Christian. It speaks of such persecutions of the Christians in Rome which contradict all that we know of Roman civilization. The abuse of Christians in the same passage may have been introduced purposely to cover up the identity of the writer. The terrible outrages against the Christians mentioned in the text from Tacitus are supposed to have taken place in the year 64 A. D. According to the New Testament, Paul was in Rome from the year 63 to the year 65, and must, therefore, have been an eye-witness of the persecution under Nero. Let me quote from the Bible to show that there could have been no such persecution as the Tacitus passage describes. The last verse in the book of Acts reads: "And he (Paul) abode two whole years in his own hired dwelling, and received all that went in unto him, preaching the kingdom of God, and teaching things concerning the Lord Jesus Christ with all boldness, *none forbidding him*." How is this picture of peace and tranquility to be reconciled with the charge that the Romans rolled up the Christians in straw mats and burned them to illuminate the streets at night, and also that the lions were let loose upon the disciples of Jesus?

Moreover, it is generally known that the Romans were indifferent to religious propaganda, and never persecuted any sect or party in the name of religion. In Rome, the Jews were free to be Jews; why should the Jewish Christians--and the early Christians were Jews--have been thrown to the lions? In all probability the persecutions were much milder than the Tacitus passage describes, and politics was the real cause.

Until not very long ago, it was universally believed that William Tell was a historical character. But it is now proven beyond any reasonable doubt, that Tell and his apple are altogether mythical. Notwithstanding that a great poet has made him the theme of a powerful drama, and a great composer devoted one of his operas to his heroic achievements; notwithstanding also that the Swiss show the crossbow with which he is supposed to have shot at the apple on his son's head--he is now admitted to be only a legendary hero. The principal arguments which have led the educated world to revise its views concerning William Tell are that, the Swiss historians, Faber and Hamurbin, who lived shortly after the "hero," and who wrote the history of their country, as Josephus did that of his, do not mention Tell. Had such a man existed before their time, they could not have failed to refer to him. Their complete silence is damaging beyond help to the historicity of Tell. Neither does the historian, who was an eye witness of the battle of Morgarten in 1315, mention the name of Tell. The Zurich Chronicle of 1497, also omits to refer to his story. In the accounts of the struggle of the Swiss against Austria, which drove the former into rebellion and ultimate independence, Tell's name cannot be found. Yet all these arguments are not half so damaging to the William Tell story, as the silence of Josephus is to the Jesus story. Jesus was supposed to have worked greater wonders and to have created a wider sensation than Tell; therefore, it is more difficult to explain the silence of historians like Josephus, Pliny and Quintilian; or of philosophers like Philo, Seneca and Epictetus, concerning Jesus, than to explain the silence of the Swiss chroniclers concerning Tell.

THE JESUS STORY A RELIGIOUS DRAMA

We have now progressed far enough in our investigation to pause a moment for reflection before we proceed any further. I am conscious of no intentional misrepresentation or suppression of the facts relating to the question in hand. If I have erred through ignorance, I shall correct any mistake I may have made, if some good reader will take the trouble to enlighten me. I am also satisfied that I have not commanded the evidence, but have allowed the evidence to command me. I am not interested in either proving or disproving the existence of the New-Testament Jesus. I am not an advocate, I am rather an umpire, who hears the evidence and pronounces his decision accordingly. Let the lawyers or the advocates argue *pro* and *con*. I only weigh,--and I am sure, impartially,--the evidence which the witnesses offer. We have heard and examined quite a number of these, and, I, at least, am compelled to say, that unless stronger evidence be forthcoming, a historical Jesus has not been proven by the evidence thus far taken in. This does not mean that there is no evidence whatever that Jesus was a real existence, but that the evidence is not enough to prove it.

To condemn or to acquit a man in a court of law, there must not only be evidence, but enough of it to justify a decision. There is some evidence for almost any imaginable proposition; but that is not enough. Not only does the evidence offered to prove Jesus' historicity, already examined, fail to give this assurance, but, on the contrary, it lends much support to the opposite supposition, namely, that in all probability, Jesus was a myth--even as Mithra, Osiris, Isis, Hercules, Sampson, Adonis, Moses, Attis, Hermes, Heracles, Apollo of Tyanna, Chrishna, and Indra, were myths.

The story of Jesus, we are constrained to say, possesses all the characteristics of the religious drama, full of startling episodes, thrilling situations, dramatic action and *denouement*. It reads more like a play than plain history. From such evidence as the gospels themselves furnish, the conclusion that he was no more than the principal character in a religious play receives much support. Mystery and morality plays are of a very ancient origin. In earlier times, almost all popular instruction was by means of *Tableaux vivant*.

As a great scenic or dramatic performance, with Jesus as the hero, Judas as the villain--with conspiracy as its plot, and the trial, the resurrection and ascension as its *finale*, the story is intelligent enough. For instance, as the curtain rises, it discloses upon the stage shepherds tending their flocks in the green fields under the moonlit sky; again, as the scene shifts, the clouds break, the heavens open, and voices are heard from above, with a white-winged chorus chanting an anthem. The next scene suggests a stable with the cattle in their stalls, munching hay. In a corner of the stable, close to a manger, imagine a young woman, stooping to kiss a newly born babe. Anon appear three bearded and richly costumed men, with presents in their hands, bowing their heads in ecstatic adoration. Surely enough this is not history: It does not read like history. The element of fiction runs through the entire Gospels, and is its warp and woof. A careful analysis of the various incidents in this *ensemble* will not fail to convince the unprejudiced reader that while they possess all the essentials for dramatic presentation, they lack the requirements of real history.

The "opened-heavens," "angel-choirs," "grazing flocks," "watchful shepherds," "worshiping magicians," "the stable crib," "the mother and child," "the wonderful star," "the presents," "the anthem"--all these, while they fit admirably as stage setting, are questionable material for history. No historical person was ever born in so spectacular a manner. The Gospel account of Jesus is an embellished, ornamental, even sensationally dramatic creation to serve as an introduction for a legendary hero. Similar theatrical furniture has been used thousands of times to introduce other legendary characters. All the Savior Gods were born supernaturally. They were all half god, half man. They were all of royal descent. Miracles and wonders attended their birth. Jesus was not an exception. We reject as mythical the birth-stories about Mithra, and Apollo. Why accept as history those about Jesus? It rests with the preachers of Christianity to show that while the god-man of Persia, or of Greece, for example, was a myth, the god-man of Palestine is historical.

The dramatic element is again plainly seen in the account of the betrayal of Jesus. Jesus, who preaches daily in the temples, and in the public places; who talks to the multitude on the mountain and at the seaside; who feeds thousands by miracle; the report of whose wonderful cures has reached the ends of the earth, and who is often followed by such a crush that to reach him an opening has to be made in the ceiling of the house where he is stopping; who goes in and out before the people and is constantly disputing with the elders and leaders of the nation--is, nevertheless, represented as being so unknown that his enemies have to resort to the device of bribing with thirty silver coins one of his disciples to point him out to them, and which is to be done by a kiss. This might make a great scene upon the stage, but it is not the way things happen in life.

Then read how Jesus is carried before Pilate the Roman governor, and how while he is being tried a courier rushes in with a letter from Pilate's wife which is dramatically torn open and read aloud in the presence of the crowded court. The letter, it is said, was about a dream of Pilate's wife, in which some ghost tells her that Jesus is innocent, and that her husband should not proceed against him. Is this history? Roman jurisprudence had not degenerated to that extent as to permit the dreams of a woman or of a man to influence the course of justice. But this letter episode was invented by the playwright--if I may use the phrase--to prolong the dramatic suspense, to complicate the situation, to twist the plot, and thereby render the impression produced by his "piece" more lasting. The letter and the dream did not save Jesus. Pilate was not influenced by his dreaming wife. She dreamed in vain.

In the next place we hear Pilate pronouncing Jesus guiltless; but, forthwith, he hands him over to the Jews to be killed. Does this read like history? Did ever a Roman court witness such a trial? To pronounce a man innocent and then to say to his prosecutors: "If you wish to kill him, you may do so," is extraordinary conduct. Then, proceeding, Pilate takes water and ostentatiously washes his hands, a proceeding introduced by a Greek or Latin scribe, who wished, in all probability, to throw the blame of the crucifixion entirely upon the Jews. Pilate, representing the Gentile world, washes his hands of the responsibility for the death of Jesus, while the Jews are made to say, "His blood be upon us and our children."

Imagine the clamoring, howling Jews, trampling on one another, gesticulating furiously, gnashing their teeth, foaming at the mouth, and spitting in one another's face as they shout, "Crucify him! Crucify him!" A very powerful stage setting, to be sure--but it is impossible to imagine that such disorder, such anarchy could be permitted in any court of justice. But think once more of those terrible words placed in the mouths of the Jews, "His blood be upon us and our children." Think of a people openly cursing themselves and asking the whole Christian world to persecute them forever--"His blood be upon *us and our children*."

Next, the composers of the gospels conduct us to the Garden of Gethsemane, that we may see there the hero of the play in his agony, fighting the great battle of his life alone, with neither help nor sympathy from his distracted followers. He is shown to us there, on his knees, crying tears of blood--sobbing and groaning under the shadow of an almost crushing fear. Tremblingly he prays, "Let this cup pass from me--if it be possible;" and then, yielding to the terror crowding in upon him, he sighs in the hearing of all the ages, "The spirit is willing, but the flesh is weak," precisely the excuse given by everybody for not doing what they would do if they could. Now, we ask in all seriousness, is it likely that a God who had come down from heaven purposely to drink that cup and to be the martyr-Savior of humanity--would seek to be spared the fate for which he was ordained from all eternity?

The objection that Jesus' hesitation on the eve of the crucifixion, as well as his cry of despair on the cross, were meant to show that he was as human as he was divine, does not solve the difficulty. In that event Jesus, then, was merely acting--feigning a fear which he did not feel, and pretending to dread a death which he knew could not hurt him. If, however, Jesus really felt alarmed at the approach of death, how much braver, then, were many of his followers who afterwards faced dangers and tortures far more cruel than his own! We honestly think that to have put in Jesus' mouth the words above quoted, and also to have represented him as closing his public career with a shriek on the cross: "My God, my God, why hast thou forsaken me?" was tantamount to an admission by the writers that they were dealing with a symbolic Christ, an ideal figure, the hero of a play, and not a historical character.

It is highly dramatic, to be sure, to see the sun darkened, to feel the whole earth quaking, to behold the graves ripped open and the dead reappear in their shrouds--to hear the hero himself tearing his own heart with that cry of shuddering anguish, "My God! my God!"--but it is not history. If such a man as Jesus really lived, then his biographers have only given us a caricature of him. However beautiful some of the sayings attributed to Jesus, and whatever the source they may have been borrowed from, they are not enough to prove his historicity. But even as the Ten Commandments do not prove Moses to have been a historical personage or the author of the books and deeds attributed to him, neither do the parables and miracles of Jesus prove him to have once visited this earth as a god, or to have even existed as a man.

Socrates and Jesus! Compare the quite natural behavior of Socrates in prison with that of Jesus in the Garden of Gethsemane. The Greek sage is serene. Jesus is alarmed. The night agony of his soul, his tears of *blood*, his pitiful collapse when he prays, "if it be possible let this cup pass from me,"--all this would be very impressive on the boards, but they seem incredible of a real man engaged in saving a world. Once more we say that the defense that it was the man in Jesus and not the god in him that broke down, would be unjust to the memory of thousands of martyrs who died by a more terrible death than that of Jesus. As elsewhere stated, but which cannot be too often emphasized, what man would not have embraced death with enthusiasm,--without a moment's misgiving, did he think that by his death, death and sin would be no more! Who would shrink from a cross which is going to save millions to millions added from eternal burnings. He must be a phantom, indeed, who trembles and cries like a frightened child because he cannot have the crown without the cross! What a spectacle for the real heroes crowding the galleries of history! It is difficult to see the shrinking and shuddering Savior of the world, his face bathed in perspiration, blood oozing out of his forehead, his lips pale, his voice breaking into a shriek, "My God, my God, why hast thou forsaken me!"--it is diffi-cult to witness all this and not to pity him. Poor Jesus! he is going to save the world, but who is going to save *him?*

If we compare the trial of Jesus with that of Socrates, the fictitious nature of the former cannot possibly escape detection. Socrates was so well known in Ath-ens, that it was not necessary for his accusers to bribe one of his disciples to betray him. Jesus should have been even better known in Jerusalem than Socrates was in Athens. He was daily preaching in the synagogues, and his miracles had given him an *eclat* which Socrates did not enjoy.

Socrates is not taken to court at night, bound hand and feet. Jesus is arrested in the glare of torchlights, after he is betrayed by Judas with a kiss; then he is bound and forced into the high priest's presence. All this is admirable setting for a stage, but they are no more than that.

The disciples of Socrates behave like real men, those of Jesus are actors. They run away; they hide and follow at a distance. One of them curses him. The cock crows, the apostate repents. This reads like a play.

In the presence of his judges, Socrates makes his own defense. One by one he meets the charges. Jesus refused, according to two of the evangelists, to open his mouth at his trial. This is dramatic, but it is not history. It is not conceivable that a real person accused as Jesus was, would have refused a great opportunity to disprove the charges against him. Socrates' defense of himself is one of the classics. Jesus' silence is a conundrum. "But he answered nothing," "But Jesus as yet answered nothing," "And he answered him never a word," is the report of two of his biographers. The other two evangelists, as is usual, contradict the former and produce the following dialogues between Jesus and his judges, which from beginning to end possess all the marks of unreality:

Pilate.--"Art thou the King of the Jews?"

Jesus.--"Sayest thou this thing of thyself, or did others tell it thee of me?"

Pilate--"Art thou a King?"

Jesus.--"Thou sayest that I am a King."

Is it possible that a real man, not to say the Savior of the world, would give such unmeaning and evasive replies to straightforward questions? Does it not read like a page from fiction?

In the presence of the priests of his own race Jesus is as indefinite and sophistical as he is before the Roman Pilate.

The Priests--"Art thou the Christ--tell us?"

Jesus.--"If I tell you ye will not believe me."

The Priests.--"Art thou the Son of God?"

Jesus.--"Ye say that I am."

In the first answer he refuses to reveal himself because he does not think he can command belief in himself; in his second answer he either blames them for saying he was the Son of God, or quotes their own testimony to prove that he is the Son of God. But if they believed he was God, would they try to kill him? Is it not unthinkable? He intimates that the priests believe he is the Son of God--"Ye say that I am." Surely, it is more probable that these dialogues were invented by his anonymous biographers than that they really represent an actual conversation between Jesus and his judges.

Compare in the next place the manner in which the public trials of Socrates and Jesus are conducted. There is order in the Athenian court; there is anarchy in the Jerusalem court. Witnesses and accusers walk up to Jesus and slap him on the face, and the judge does not reprove them for it. The court is in the hands of rowdies and hoodlums, who shout "Crucify him," and again, "Crucify him." A Roman judge, while admitting that he finds no guilt in Jesus deserving of death, is nevertheless represented as handing him over to the mob to be killed, after he has himself scourged him. No Roman judge could have behaved as this Pilate is reported to have behaved toward an accused person on trial for his life. All that we know of civilized government, all that we know of the jurisprudence of Rome, contradicts this "inspired" account of a pretended historical event. If Jesus was ever tried and condemned to death in a Roman court, an account of it that can command belief has yet to be written.

Again, when we come to consider the random, disconnected and fragmentary form in which the teachings of Jesus are presented, we cannot avoid the conclusion that he is a ***dramatis persona*** brought upon the stage to give expression not to a consistent, connected and carefully worked-out thought, but to voice with many breaks and interruptions, the ideas of his changing managers. He is made to play a number of contradictory roles, and appears in the same story in totally different characters.

One editor or compiler of the Gospel describes Jesus as an ascetic and a mendicant, wandering from place to place, without a roof over his head, and crawling at eventide into his cave in the Mount of Olives. He introduces him as the "Man of Sorrows," fasting in the wilderness, counseling people to part with their riches, and promising the Kingdom of Heaven to Lazarus, the beggar.

Another redactor announces him as "eating and drinking" at the banquets of "publicans and sinners,"--a "wine-bibbing" Son of Man. "John the Baptist came neither eating nor drinking, but the Son of Man came both eating and drinking," which, if it means anything, means that Jesus was the very opposite of the ascetic John.

A partisan of the doctrine of non-resistance puts in Jesus' mouth the words: "Resist not evil;" "The meek shall inherit the earth," etc., and counsels that he who smites us on the one cheek should be permitted to strike us also on the other, and that to him who robs us of an undergarment, we should also hand over our outer garments.

Another draws the picture of a militant Jesus who could never endorse such precepts of indolence and resignation. "The kingdom of heaven is taken by ***violence***," cries this new Jesus, and intimates that no such beggar like Lazarus, sitting all day long with the dogs and his sores, can ever earn so great a prize. With a scourge in his hands this Jesus rushes upon the traders in the temple-court, upturns their tables and whips their owners into the streets. Surely this was resistance of the most pronounced type. The right to use physical force could not have been given a better endorsement than by this example of Jesus.

It will not help matters to say that these money-changers were violating a divine law, and needed chastisement with a whip. Is not the man who smites us upon the cheek, or robs us of our clothing, equally guilty? Moreover, these traders in the outer courts of the synagogue were rendering the worshipers a useful service. Just as candles, rosaries, images and literature are sold in church vestibules for the accommodation of Catholics, so were doves, pigeons and Hebrew coins, necessary to the Jewish sacrifices, sold in the temple-courts for the Jewish worshiper. The money changer who supplied the pious Jew with the only sacred coin which the priests would accept was not very much less important to the Jewish religion than the rabbi. To have fallen upon these traders with a weapon, and to have caused them the loss of their property, was certainly the most inconsistent thing that a "meek" and "lowly" Jesus preaching non-resistance could have done.

Again; one writer makes Jesus the teacher *par excellence* of peace. He counsels forgiveness of injuries not seven times, but seventy times that number--meaning unlimited love and charity. "Love your enemies," "Bless them that curse you," is his unusual advice. But another hand retouches this picture, and we have a Jesus who breaks his own golden rule. This other Jesus heaps abuse upon the people who displease him; calls his enemies "vipers," "serpents," "devils," and predicts for them eternal burnings in sulphur and brimstone. How could he who said, "Come unto me all ye that are heavy laden," say also, "Depart from me ye *cursed*?" Who curses them? How can there be an everlasting hell in a universe whose author advises us to love our enemies, to bless them that curse us, and to forgive seventy times seven? How could the same Jesus who said, "Blessed are the peacemakers," say also, "I came not to bring peace, but a sword?" Is it possible that the same Jesus who commands us to love our *enemies*, commands us also to "hate" father, mother, wife and child, for "his name's sake?" Yes! the same Jesus who said, "Put up thy sword in its sheath," also commands us to sell our effects and "buy a sword."

Once more: A believer in the divinity of Jesus--I am going to say--invents the following text: "The Father and I are *one*." An opponent to this Trinitarian dogma introduces a correction which robs the above text of its authority: "The Father is greater than I," and makes Jesus admit openly that there are some things known to the father only. It is difficult not to see in these passages the beginnings of the terrible controversies which, starting with Peter and Paul, have come down to our day, ***and which will not end*** until Jesus shall take his place among the mythical saviors of the world.

To harmonize these many and different Jesuses into something like unity or consistency a thousand books have been written by the clergy. They have not succeeded. How can a Jesus represented at one time as the image of divine perfection, and at another as protesting against being called "good," for "none is good, save one, God,"--how can these two conceptions be reconciled except by a resort to artificial and arbitrary interpretations? If such insurmountable contradictions in the teachings and character of another would weaken our faith in his historicity, then we are justified in inferring that in all probability Jesus was only a name--the name of an imaginary stage hero, uttering the conflicting thoughts of his prompters.

Again, such phrases as, "and he was caught up in a cloud,"--describing the ascension and consequent disappearance of Jesus, betray the anxiety of the authors of the Gospels to bring their marvelous story to a close. Not knowing how to terminate the career of an imaginary Messiah, his creators invented the above method of dispatching him. "He was caught up in a cloud,"--but for that, the narrators would have been obliged to continue their story indefinitely.

In tragedy the play ends with the death of the hero, but if the biographers of Jesus had given a similar excuse for bringing their narrative to a ***finale***, there would have been the danger of their being asked to point out his grave. "He was caught up in a cloud," relieved them of all responsibility to produce his remains if called upon to do so, and, at the same time, furnished them with an excuse to bring their story to a close.

It would hardly be necessary, were we all unbiased, to look for any further proofs of the mythical and fanciful nature of the Gospel narratives than this expedient to which the writers resorted. To questions, "Where is Jesus?" "What became of his body?" etc., they could answer, "He was caught up in a cloud." But a career that ends in the clouds was never begun on the earth.

Let us imagine ourselves in Jerusalem in the year One, of the Christian era, when the apostles, as it is claimed, were proclaiming Jesus as the Messiah, crucified and risen. Desiring to be convinced before believing in the strange story, let us suppose the following conversation between the apostles and ourselves. We ask:

How long have you known Jesus?

I have known him for one year.

And I for two.

And I for three.

Has any of you known him for more than three years?

No.

Was he with his apostles for one year or for three?

For one.

No, for three.

You are not certain, then, how long Jesus was with his apostles.

No.

How old was Jesus when crucified?

About thirty-one.

No, about thirty-three.

No, he was much older, about fifty.

You cannot tell with any certainty, then, his age at the time of his death.

No.

You say he was tried and crucified in Jerusalem before your own eyes, can you remember the date of this great event?

We cannot.

Were you present when Jesus was taken down from the cross?

We were not.

You cannot tell, then, whether he was dead when taken down.

We have no personal knowledge.

Were you present when he was buried?

We were not, because we were in hiding for our lives.

You do not know, therefore, whether he was actually buried, or where he was buried.

We do not.

Were any of you present when Jesus came forth from the grave?

Not one of us was present,

Then, you were not with him when he was taken down from the cross; you were not with him when he was interred, and you were not present when he rose from the grave.

We were not.

When, therefore, you say, he was dead, buried and rose again, you are relying upon the testimony of others?

We are.

Will you mention the names of some of the witnesses who saw Jesus come forth from the tomb?

Mary Magdalene, and she is here and may be questioned.

Were you present, Mary, when the angels rolled away the stone, and when Jesus came forth from the dead?

No, when I reached the burying place early in the morning, the grave had already been vacated, and there was no one sleeping in it.

You saw him, then, as the apostles did, *after* he had risen?

Yes.

But you did not see anybody rise out of the grave.

I did not.

Are there any witnesses who saw the resurrection?

There are many who saw him after the resurrection.

But if neither they nor you saw him dead, and buried, and did not see him rise, either, how can you tell that a most astounding and supposedly impossible miracle had taken place between the time you saw him last and when you saw him again two or three days after? Is it not more natural to suppose that, being in a hurry on account of the approaching Sabbath, Jesus, if ever crucified, was taken down from the cross before he had really died, and that he was not buried, as rumor states, but remained in hiding; and his showing himself to you under cover of darkness and in secluded spots and in the dead of night only, would seem to confirm this explanation.

You admit also that the risen Jesus did not present himself at the synagogues of the people, in the public streets, or at the palace of the High Priest to convince them of his Messiahship. Do you not think that if he had done this, it would then have been impossible to deny his resurrection? Why, then, did Jesus hide himself after he came out of the grave? Why did he not show himself also to his enemies? Was he still afraid of them, or did he not care whether they believed or not? If so, why are *you* trying to convert them? The question waits for a reasonable answer; Why did not Jesus challenge the whole world with the evidence of his resurrection? You say you saw him occasionally, a few moments at a time, now here, and now there, and finally on the top of a mountain whence he was caught up in a cloud and disappeared altogether. But that "cloud" has melted away, the sky is clear, and there is no Jesus visible there. The cloud, then, had nothing to hide. It was unnecessary to call in a cloud to close the career of your Christ. The grave is empty, the cloud has vanished. Where is Christ? In heaven! Ah, you have at last removed him to a world unknown, to the undiscovered country. Leave him there! Criticism, doubt, investigation, the light of day, cannot cross its shores. Leave him there!

THE JESUS OF PAUL

The central figure of the New Testament is Jesus, and the question we are trying to answer is, whether we have sufficient evidence to prove to the unbiased mind that he is historical. An idea of the intellectual caliber of the average churchman may be had by the nature of the evidence he offers to justify his faith in the historical Jesus. "The whole world celebrates annually the nativity of Jesus; how could there be a Christmas celebration if there never was a Christ?" asks a Chicago clergyman. The simplicity of this plea would be touching were it not that it calls attention to the painful inefficiency of the pulpit as an educator. The church goer is trained to believe, not to think. The truth is withheld from him under the pious pretense that faith, and not knowledge, is the essential thing. A habit of untruthfulness is cultivated by systematically sacrificing everything to orthodoxy. This habit in the end destroys one's conscience for any truths which are prejudicial to one's interest. But is it true that the Christmas celebration proves a historical Jesus?

We can only offer a few additional remarks to what we have already said elsewhere in these pages on the Pagan origin of Christmas. It will make us grateful to remember that just as we have to go to the Pagans for the origins of our civilized institutions--our courts of justice, our art and literature, and our political and religious liberties--we must thank them also for our merry festivals, such as Christmas and Easter. The ignorant, of course, do not know anything about the value and wealth of the legacy bequeathed to us by our glorious ancestors of Greek and Roman times, but the educated can have no excuse for any failure to own their everlasting indebtedness to the Pagans. It will be impossible today to write the history of civilization without giving to the classical world the leading role. But while accepting the gifts of the Pagan peoples we have abused the givers. A beneficiary who will defame a bounteous benefactor is unworthy of his good fortune. I regret to say that the Christian church, notwithstanding that it owes many of its most precious privileges to the Pagans, has returned for service rendered insolence and vituperation. No generous or just institution would treat a rival as Christianity has treated Paganism.

Both Christmas and Easter are Pagan festivals. We do not know, no one knows, when Jesus was born; but we know the time of the winter solstice when the sun begins to retrace his steps, turning his radiant face toward our earth once more. It was this event, a natural, demonstrable, universal, event, that our European ancestors celebrated with song and dance--with green branches, through which twinkled a thousand lighted candles, and with the exchange of good wishes and gifts. Has the church had the courage to tell its people that Christmas is a Pagan festival which was adopted and adapted by the Christian world, reluctantly at first, and in the end as a measure of compromise only? The Protestants, especially, conveniently forget the severe Puritanic legislation against the observance of this Pagan festival, both in England and America. It is the return to Paganism which has given to Christmas and Easter their great popularity, as it is the revival of Paganism which is everywhere replacing the Bible ideas of monarchic government with republicanism. And yet, repeatedly, and without any scruples of conscience, preacher and people claim these festivals as the gifts of their creed to humanity, and quote them further to prove the historical existence of their god-man, Jesus. It was this open and persistent perversion of history by the church, the manufacture of evidence on the one hand, the suppression of witnesses prejudiced to her interests on the other, and the deliberate forging of documents, which provoked Carlyle into referring to one of its branches as *the great lying Church*.

We have said enough to show that, in all probability--for let us not be dogmatic--the story of Jesus,--his birth and betrayal by one of his own disciples, his trial in a Roman court, his crucifixion, resurrection and ascension,--belongs to the order of imaginative literature. Conceived at first as a religious drama, it received many new accretions as it traveled from country to country and from age to age. The "piece" shows signs of having been touched and retouched to make it acceptable to the different countries in which it was played. The hand of the adapter, the interpolator and the reviser is unmistakably present. As an allegory, or as a dramatic composition, meant for the religious stage, it proved one of the strongest productions of Pagan or Christian times. But as real history, it lacks the fundamental requisite--probability. As a play, it is stirring and strong; as history, it lacks naturalness and consistency. The miraculous is ever outside the province of history. Jesus was a miracle, and as such, at least, we are safe in declaring him un- historical.

We pass on now to the presentation of evidence which we venture to think demonstrates with an almost mathematic precision, that the Jesus of the four gospels is a legendary hero, as unhistorical as William Tell of Switzerland. This evidence is furnished by the epistles bearing the signature of Paul. He has been accepted as not only the greatest apostle of Christianity, but in a sense also the author of its theology. It is generally admitted that the epistles bearing the name of Paul are among the oldest apostolical writings. They are older than the gospels. This is very important information. When Paul was preaching, the four gospels had not yet been written. From the epistles of Paul, of which there are about thirteen in the Bible--making the New Testament largely the work of this one apostle--we learn that there were in different parts of Asia, a number of Christian churches already established. Not only Paul, then, but also the Christian church was in existence before the gospels were composed. It would be natural to infer that it was not the gospels which created the church, but the church which produced the gospels. Do not lose sight of the fact that when Paul was preaching to the Christians there was no written biography of Jesus in existence. There was a church without a book.

In comparing the Jesus of Paul with the Jesus whose portrait is drawn for us in the gospels, we find that they are not the same persons at all. This is decisive. Paul knows nothing about a miraculously born savior. He does not mention a single time, in all his thirteen epistles, that Jesus was born of a virgin, or that his birth was accompanied with heavenly signs and wonders. He knew nothing of a Jesus born after the manner of the gospel writers. It is not imaginable that he knew the facts, but suppressed them, or that he considered them unimportant, or that he forgot to refer to them in any of his public utterances. Today, a preacher is expelled from his denomination if he suppresses or ignores the miraculous conception of the Son of God; but Paul was guilty of that very heresy. How explain it? It is quite simple: The virgin-born Jesus was not yet *invented* when Paul was preaching Christianity. Neither he, nor the churches he had organized, had ever heard of such a person. The virgin-born Jesus was of later origin than the Apostle Paul.

Let the meaning of this discrepancy between the Jesus of Paul, that is to say, the earliest portrait of Jesus, and the Jesus of the four evangelists, be fully grasped by the student, and it should prove beyond a doubt that in Paul's time the story of Jesus' birth from the virgin-mother and the Holy Ghost, which has since become a cardinal dogma of the Christian church, was not yet in circulation. Jesus had not yet been Hellenized; he was still a Jewish Messiah whose coming was foretold in the Old Testament, and who was to be a prophet like unto Moses, without the remotest suggestion of a supernatural origin.

No proposition in Euclid is safer from contradiction than that, if Paul knew what the gospels tell about Jesus, he would have, at least once or twice during his long ministry, given evidence of his knowledge of it. The conclusion is inevitable that the gospel Jesus is later than Paul and his churches. Paul stood nearest to the time of Jesus. Of those whose writings are supposed to have come down to us, he is the most representative, and his epistles are the *first* literature of the new religion. And yet there is absolutely not a single hint or suggestion in them of such a Jesus as is depicted in the gospels. The gospel Jesus was not yet put together or compiled, when Paul was preaching.

Once more; if we peruse carefully and critically the writings of Paul, the earliest and greatest Christian apostle and missionary, we find that he is not only ignorant of the gospel stories about the birth and miracles of Jesus, but he is equally and just as innocently ignorant of the *teachings* of Jesus. In the gospels Jesus is the author of the Sermon on the Mount, the Lord's Prayer, the Parable of the Prodigal Son, the Story of Dives, the Good Samaritan, etc. Is it conceivable that a preacher of Jesus could go throughout the world to convert people to the teachings of Jesus, as Paul did, without ever quoting a single one of his sayings? Had Paul known that

Jesus had preached a sermon, or formulated a prayer, or said many inspired things about the here and the hereafter, he could not have helped quoting, now and then, from the words of his master. If Christianity could have been established without a knowledge of the teachings of Jesus, why, then, did Jesus come to teach, and why were his teachings preserved by divine inspiration? But if a knowledge of these teachings of Jesus is indispensable to making converts, Paul gives not the least evidence that he possessed such knowledge.

But the Apostle Paul, judging from his many epistles to the earliest converts to Christianity, which are really his testimony, supposed to have been sealed by his blood, appears to be quite as ignorant of a Jesus who went about working miracles,--opening the eyes of the blind, giving health to the sick, hearing to the deaf, and life to the dead,--as he is of a Jesus born of a virgin woman and the Holy Ghost. Is not this remarkable? Does it not lend strong confirmation to the idea that the miracle-working Jesus of the gospels was not known in Paul's time, that is to say, the earliest Jesus known to the churches was a person altogether different from his namesake in the four evangelists. If Paul knew of a miracle-working Jesus, one who could feed the multitude with a few loaves and fishes--who could command the grave to open, who could cast out devils, and cleanse the land of the foulest disease of leprosy, who could, and did, perform many other wonderful works to convince the unbelieving generation of his divinity,--is it conceivable that either intentionally or inadvertently he would have never once referred to them in all his preaching? Is it not almost certain that, if the earliest Christians knew of the miracles of Jesus, they would have been greatly surprised at the failure of Paul to refer to them a single time? And would not Paul have told them of the promise of Jesus to give them power to work even greater miracles than his own, had he known of such a promise. Could Paul really have left out of his ministry so essential a chapter from the life of Jesus, had he been acquainted with it? The miraculous fills up the greater portion of the four gospels, and if these documents were dictated by the Holy Ghost, it means that they were too important to be left out. Why, then, does not Paul speak of them at all? There is only one reasonable answer: A miracle-working Jesus was unknown to Paul.

What would we say of a disciple of Tolstoi, for example, who came to America to make converts to Count Tolstoi and never once quoted anything that Tolstoi had said? Or what would we think of the Christian missionaries who go to India, China, Japan and Africa to preach the gospel, if they never mentioned to the people of these countries the Sermon on the Mount, the Parable of the Prodigal Son, the Lord's Prayer--nor quoted a single text from the gospels? Yet Paul, the first missionary, did the very thing which would be inexplicable in a modern missionary. There is only one rational explanation for this: The Jesus of Paul was not born of a virgin; he did not work miracles; and he was not a teacher. It was after his day that such a Jesus was--I have to use again a strong word--***invented***.

It has been hinted by certain professional defenders of Christianity that Paul's specific mission was to introduce Christianity among the Gentiles, and not to call attention to the miraculous element in the life of his Master. But this is a very lame defense. What is Christianity, but the life and teachings of Jesus? And how can it be introduced among the Gentiles without a knowledge of the doctrines and works of its founder? Paul gives no evidence of possessing any knowledge of the teachings of Jesus, how could he, then, be a missionary of Christianity to the heathen? There is no other answer which can be given than that the Christianity of Paul was something radically different from the Christianity of the later gospel writers, who in all probability were Greeks and not Jews. Moreover, it is known that Paul was reprimanded by his fellow-apostles for carrying Christianity to the Gentiles. What better defense could Paul have given for his conduct than to have quoted the commandment of Jesus--

"Go ye into all the world and preach the gospel to every creature." And he would have quoted the "divine" text had he been familiar with it. Nay, the other apostles would not have taken him to task for obeying the commandment of Jesus had they been familiar with such a commandment. It all goes to support the proposition that the gospel Jesus was of a date later than the apostolic times.

That the authorities of the church realize how damaging to the reality of the gospel Jesus is the inexplicable silence of Paul concerning him, may be seen in their vain effort to find in a passage put in Paul's mouth by the unknown author of the book of ***Acts***, evidence that Paul does quote the sayings of Jesus. The passage referred to is the following: "It is more blessed to give than to receive." Paul is made to state that this was a saying of Jesus. In the first place, this quotation is not in the epistles of Paul, but in the ***Acts***, of which Paul was not the author; in the second place, there is no such quotation in the gospels. The position, then, that there is not a single saying of Jesus in the gospels which is quoted by Paul in his many epistles is unassailable, and certainly fatal to the historicity of the gospel Jesus.

Again, from Paul himself we learn that he was a zealous Hebrew, a Pharisee of Pharisees, studying with Gamaliel in Jerusalem, presumably to become a rabbi. Is it possible that such a man could remain totally ignorant of a miracle worker and teacher like Jesus, living in the same city with him? If Jesus really raised Lazarus from the grave, and entered Jerusalem at the head of a procession, waving branches and shouting, "hosanna"--if he was really crucified in Jerusalem, and ascended from one of its environs--is it possible that Paul neither saw Jesus nor heard anything about these miracles? But if he knew all these things about Jesus, is it possible that he could go through the world preaching Christ without ever once referring to them? It is more likely that when Paul was studying in Jerusalem there was no miraculous Jesus living or teaching in any part of Judea.

If men make their gods they also make their Christs. [Note: Christianity and Mythology. J. M. Robertson, to whom the author acknowledges his indebtedness, for the difference between Paul's Jesus and that of the Gospels.] It is frequently urged that it was impossible for a band of illiterate fishermen to have created out of their own fancy so glorious a character as that of Jesus, and that it would be more miraculous to suppose that the unique sayings of Jesus and his incomparably perfect life were invented by a few plain people than to believe in his actual existence. But it is not honest to throw the question into that form. We do not know who were the authors of the gospels. It is pure assumption that they were written by plain fishermen. The authors of the gospels do not disclose their identity. The words, *according* to Matthew, Mark, etc., represent only the guesses or opinions of translators and copyists.

Both in the gospels and in Christian history the apostles are represented as illiterate men. But if they spoke Greek, and could also write in Greek, they could not have been just plain fishermen. That they were Greeks, not Jews, and more or less educated, may be safely inferred from the fact that they all write in Greek, and one of them at least seems to be acquainted with the Alexandrian school of philosophy. Jesus was supposedly a Jew, his twelve apostles all Jews--how is it, then, that the only biographies of him extant are all in Greek? If his fishermen disciples were capable of composition in Greek, they could not have been illiterate men, if they could not have written in Greek--which was a rare accomplishment for a Jew, according to what Josephus says--then the gospels were not written by the apostles of Jesus. But the fact that though these documents are in a language alien both to Jesus and his disciples, they are unsigned and undated, goes to prove, we think, that their editors or authors wished to conceal their identity that they may be taken for the apostles themselves.

In the next place it is equally an assumption that the portrait of Jesus is incomparable. It is now proven beyond a doubt that there is not a single saying of Jesus, I say this deliberately, which had not already been known both among the Jews and Pagans. [Note: Sometimes it is urged by pettifogging clergymen that, while it is true that Confucius gave the Golden Rule six hundred years before Jesus, it was in a negative form. Confucius said, "Do not unto another what you would not another to do unto you." Jesus said, "Do unto others," etc. But every negative has its corresponding affirmation. Moreover, are not the Ten Commandments in the negative? But the Greek sages gave the Golden Rule in as positive a form as we find it in the Gospels. "And may I do to others as I would that others should do to me," said Plato.--Jowett Trans., V.--483. P.

Besides, if the only difference between Jesus and Confucius, the one a God, the other a mere man, was that they both said the same thing, the one in the negative, the other in the positive, it is not enough to prove Jesus infinitely superior to Confucius. Many of Jesus' own commandments are in the negative: "Resist not evil," for instance.] And as to his life; it is in no sense superior or even as large and as many sided as that of Socrates. I know some consider it blasphemy to compare Jesus with Socrates, but that must be attributed to prejudice rather than to reason.

And to the question that if Jesus be mythical, we cannot account for the rise and progress of the Christian church, we answer that the Pagan gods who occupied Mount Olympus were all mythical beings--mere shadows, and yet Paganism was the religion of the most advanced and cultured nations of antiquity. How could an imaginary Zeus, or Jupiter, draw to his temple the elite of Greece and Rome? And if there is nothing strange in the rise and spread of the Pagan church; in the rapid progress of the worship of Osiris, who never existed; in the wonderful success of the religion of Mithra, who is but a name; if the worship of Adonis, of Attis, of Isis, and the legends of Heracles, Prometheus, Hercules, and the Hindoo trinity,--Brahma, Shiva, Chrishna,--with their rock-hewn temples, can be explained without believing in the actual existence of these gods--why not Christianity? Religions, like everything else, are born, they grow old and die. They show the handiwork of whole races, and of different epochs, rather than of one man or of one age. Time gives them birth, and changing environments determine their career. Just as the portrait of Jesus we see in shops and churches is an invention, so is his character. The artist gave him his features, the theologian his attributes.

What are the elements out of which the Jesus story was evolved? The Jewish people were in constant expectation of a Messiah. The belief prevailed that his name would be Joshua, which in English is Jesus. The meaning of the word is *savior*. In ancient Syrian mythology, Joshua was a Sun God. The Old-Testament Joshua, who "stopped the Sun," was in all probability this same Syrian divinity. According to tradition this Joshua, or Jesus, was the son of Mary, a name which with slight variations. is found in nearly all the old mythologies. Greek and Hindoo divinities were mothered by either a Mary, Meriam, Myrrah, or Merri. Maria or Mares is the oldest word for sea--the earliest source of life. The ancients looked upon the sea-water as the mother of every living thing. "Joshua (or Jesus), son of Mary," was already a part of the religious outfit of the Asiatic world when Paul began his missionary tours. His Jesus, or anointed one, crucified or slain, did in no sense represent a new or original message. It is no more strange that Paul's mythological "savior" should loom into prominence and cast a spell over all the world, than that a mythical Apollo or Jupiter should rule for thousands of years over the fairest portions of the earth.

It is also well known that there is in the Talmud the story of a Jesus, Ben, or son, of Pandira, who lived about a hundred years before the Gospel Jesus, and who was hanged from a tree. I believe this Jesus is quite as legendary as the Syrian Hesous, or Joshua. But may it not be that such a legend accepted as true--to the ancients all legends were true--contributed its share toward marking the outlines of the later Jesus, hanged on a cross? My idea has been to show that the materials for a Jesus myth were at hand, and that, therefore, to account for the rise and progress of the Christian cult is no more difficult than to explain the widely spread religion of the Indian Chrishna, or of the Persian Mithra. [Note: For a fuller discussion of the various "christs" in mythology read Robertson's Christianity and Mythology and his Pagan Christs.]

Now, why have I given these conclusions to the world? Would I not have made more friends--provoked a warmer response from the public at large--had I repeated in pleasant accents the familiar phrases about the glory and beauty and sweetness of the Savior God, the Virgin-born Christ? Instead of that, I have run the risk of alienating the sympathies of my fellows by intimating that this Jesus whom Christendom worships today as a god, this Jesus at whose altar the Christian world bends its knees and bows its head, is as much of an idol as was Apollo of the Greeks; and that we--we Americans of the twentieth century--are an idolatrous people, inasmuch as we worship a name, or at most, a man of whom we know nothing provable.

IS CHRISTIANITY REAL?

It is assumed, without foundation, as I hope to show, that the religion of Jesus alone can save the world. We are not surprised at the claim, because there has never been a religion which has been too modest to make a similar claim. No religion has ever been satisfied to be *one* of the saviors of man. Each religion wants to be the *only* savior of man. There is no monopoly like religious monopoly. The industrial corporations with all their greed are less exacting than the Catholic church, for instance, which keeps heaven itself under lock and key.

But what is meant by salvation? Let us consider its religious meaning first. An unbiased investigation of the dogmas and their supposed historical foundations will prove that the salvation which Christianity offers, and the means by which it proposes to effect the world's salvation, are extremely fanciful in nature. If this point could be made clear, there will be less reluctance on the part of the public to listen to the evidence on the un-historicity of the founder of Christianity.

We are told that God, who is perfect, created this world about half a hundred centuries ago. Of course, being perfect himself the world which he created was perfect, too. But the world did not stay perfect very long. Nay, from the heights it fell, not slowly, but suddenly, into the lowest depths of degradation. How a world which God had created perfect, could in the twinkling of an eye become so vile as to be cursed by the same being who a moment before had pronounced it "good," and besides be handed over to the devil as fuel for eternal burnings, only credulity can explain. I am giving the story of what is called the "plan of salvation," in order to show its mythical nature. In the preceding pages we have discussed the question, Is Jesus a Myth, but I believe that when we have reflected upon the story of man's fall and his supposed subsequent salvation by the blood of Jesus, we shall conclude that the function, or the office, which Jesus is said to perform, is as mythical as his person.

The story of Eden possesses all the marks of an allegory. Adam and Eve, and a perfect world *suddenly* plunged from a snowy whiteness into the blackness of hell, are the thoughts of a child who exaggerates because of an as yet undisciplined fancy. Yet, if Adam and Eve are unreal, theologically speaking, Jesus is unreal. If they are allegory and myth, so is Jesus. It is claimed that it was the fall of Adam which necessitated the death of Jesus, but if Adam's fall be a fiction, as we know it is, Jesus' death as an atonement must also be a fiction.

In the fall of Adam, we are told, humanity itself fell. Could anything be more fanciful than that? And what was Adam's sin? He coveted knowledge. He wished to improve his mind. He experimented with forbidden things. He dared to take the initiative. And for that imaginary crime, even the generations not yet born are to be forever blighted. Even the animals, the flowers and vegetables were cursed for it. Can you conceive of anything more mythical than that? One of the English divines of the age of Calvin declared that original sin,--Adam's sin imputed to us,--was so awful, that "if a man had never been born he would yet have been damned for it." It is from this mythical sin that a mythical Savior saves us. And how does he do it? In a very mythical way, as we shall see.

When the world fell, it fell into the devil's hands. To redeem a part of it, at least, the deity concludes to give up his only son for a ransom. This is interesting. God is represented as being greatly offended, because the world which he had created perfect was all in a heap before him. To placate himself he sacrificed his son--not himself.

But, as intimated above, he does not intend to restore the whole world to its pristine purity, but only a part of it. This is alarming. He creates the whole world perfect, but now he is satisfied to have only a portion of it redeemed from the devil. If he can save at all, pray, why not save all? This is not an irrelevant question when it is remembered that the whole world was created perfect in the first place.

The refusal of the deity to save all of his world from the devil would lead one to believe that even when God created the world perfect he did not mean to keep all of it to himself, but meant that some of it, the greater part of it, as some theologians contend, should go to the devil! Surely this is nothing but myth. Let us hope for the sake of our ideals that all this is no more than the childish prattle of primitive man.

But let us return to the story of the fall of man; God decides to save a part of his ruined perfect world by the sacrifice of his son. The latter is supposed to have said to his father: "Punish me, kill me, accept my blood, and let it pay for the sins of man." He thus interceded for the *elect*, and the deity was mollified. As Jesus is also God, it follows that one God tried to pacify another, which is pure myth. Some theologians have another theory--there is room here for many theories. According to these, God gave up his son as a ransom, not to himself, but to the devil, who now claimed the world as his own. I heard a distinguished minister explain this in the following manner: A poor man whose house is mortgaged hears that some philanthropist has redeemed the property by paying off the mortgage. The soul of man was by the fall of Adam mortgaged to the devil. God has raised the mortgage by abandoning his son to be killed to satisfy the devil who held the mortgage. The debt which we owed has been paid by Jesus. By this arrangement the devil loses his legal right to our souls and we are saved. All we need to do is to believe in this story and we'll be sure to go to heaven. And to think that intelligent Americans not only accept all this as inspired, but denounce the man who ventures to intimate modestly that it might be a myth, as a blasphemer! "O, judgment!" cries Shakespeare, "thou hast fled to brutish beasts, and men have lost their reason."

The morality which the Christian church teaches is of as mythical a nature as the story of the fall, and the blood-atonement. It is not natural morality, but something quite unintelligible and fictitious. For instance, we are told that we cannot of ourselves be righteous. We must first have the grace of God. Then we are told that we cannot have the grace of God unless he gives it to us. And he will not give it to us unless we ask for it. But we cannot ask for it, unless he moves us to ask for it. And there we are. We shall be damned if we do not come to God, and we cannot come to God unless he calls us. Besides, could anything be more mythical than a righteousness which can only be imputed to us,--any righteousness of our own being but "filthy rags?"

The Christian religion has the appearance of being one great myth, constructed out of many minor myths. It is the same with Mohammedanism, or Judaism, which latter is the mischievous parent of both the Mohammedan and the Christian faiths. It is the same with all supernatural creeds. Myth is the dominating element in them all. Compared with these Asiatic religions how glorious is science! How wholesome, helpful, and luminous, are her commandments!

If I were to command you to believe that Mount Olympus was once tenanted by blue-eyed gods and their consorts,--sipping nectar and ambrosia the live-long day,--you will answer, "Oh, that is only mythology." If I were to tell you that you cannot be saved unless you believe that Minerva was born full-fledged from the brain of Jupiter, you will laugh at me. If I were to tell you that you must punish your innocent sons for the guilt of their brothers and sisters, you will answer that I insult your moral sense. And yet, every Sunday, the preacher repeats the myth of Adam and Eve, and how God killed his innocent son to please himself, or to satisfy the devil, and with bated breath, and on your knees, you whisper, **Amen.**

How is it that when you read the literature of the Greeks, the literature of the Persians, the literature of Hindoostan, or of the Mohammedan world, you discriminate between fact and fiction, between history and myth, but when it comes to the literature of the Jews, you stammer, you stutter, you bite your lips, you turn pale, and fall upon your face before it as the savage before his fetish? You would consider it unreasonable to believe that everything a Greek, or a Roman, or an Arab ever said was inspired. And yet, men have been hounded to death for not believing that everything that a Jew ever said in olden times was inspired.

I do not have to use arguments, I hope, to prove to an intelligent public that an infallible book is as much a myth as the Garden of Eden, or the Star of Bethlehem.

A mythical Savior, a mythical Bible, a mythical plan of salvation!

When we subject what are called religious truths to the same tests by which we determine scientific or historical truths, we discover that they are not truths at all; they are only opinions. Any statement which snaps under the strain of reason is unworthy of credence. But it is claimed that religious truth is discovered by intuition and not by investigation. The believer, it is claimed, feels in his own soul--he has the witness of the spirit, that the Bible is infallible, and that Jesus is the Savior of man. The Christian does not have to look into the arguments for or against his religion, it is said, before he makes up his mind; he knows by an inward assurance; he has proved it to his own deepermost being that Jesus is real and that he is the only Savior. But what is that but another kind of argument? The argument is quite inadequate to inspire assurance, as you will presently see, but it is an argument nevertheless. To say that we must believe and not reason is a kind of reasoning, This device of reasoning against reasoning is resorted to by people who have been compelled by modern thought to give up, one after another, the strongholds of their position. They run under shelter of what they call faith, or the "inward witness of the spirit," or the intuitive argument, hoping thereby to escape the enemy's fire, if I may use so objectionable a phrase.

What is called faith, then, or an intuitive spiritual assurance, is a species of reasoning; let its worth be tested honestly.

In the first place, faith or the intuitive argument would prove too much. If Jesus is real, notwithstanding that there is no reliable historical data to warrant the belief, because the believer feels in his own soul that He is real and divine, I answer that, the same mode of reasoning--and let us not forget, it is a kind of *reasoning*--would prove Mohammed a divine savior, and the wooden idol of the savage a god. The African Bushman trembles before an image, because he feels in his own soul that the thing is real. Does that make it real? The Moslem cries unto Mohammed, because he believes in his innermost heart that Mohammed is near and can hear him. He will risk his life on that assurance. To quote to him history and science to prove that Mohammed is dead and unable to save, would be of no avail, for he has the witness of the spirit in him, an intuitive assurance, that the great prophet sits on the right hand of Allah. An argument which proves too much, proves nothing.

In the second place, an intuition is not communicable. I may have an intuition that I see spirits all about me this morning. They come, they go, they nod, they brush my forehead with their wings. But do *you* see them, too, because I see them? There is the difference between a scientific demonstration and a purely metaphysical assumption. I could go to the blackboard and assure you, as I am myself assured, that two parallel lines running in the same direction will not and cannot meet. That is demonstration. A fever patient when in a state of delirium, and a frightened child in the dark, see things. We do not deny that they do, but their testimony does not prove that the things they see are real.

"What is this I see before me?" cries Macbeth, the murderer, and he shrieks and shakes from head to foot--he draws his sword and rushes upon Banquo's ghost, which he sees coldly staring at him. But is that any proof that what he saw we could see also? Yes, we could, if we were in the same frenzy! And it is the revivalist's aim, by creating a general excitement, to make everybody *see things*. "Doctor, Doctor, help! they are coming to kill me; there they are--the assassins,--one, two, three-- oh, help," and the patient jumps out of bed to escape the banditti crowding in upon him. But is that any reason why the attending physician, his pulse normal and his brow cool, should believe that the room is filling up with assassins? I observe people jump up and down, as they do in holiness meetings; I hear them say they see angels, they see Jesus, they feel his presence. But is that any evidence for you or me? An intuitive argument is not communicable, and, therefore, it is no argument at all.

Our orthodox friends are finally driven by modern thought, which is growing bolder every day, to the only refuge left for them. It is the one already mentioned. Granted that Jesus was an imaginary character, even then, as an ideal, they argue, he is an inspiration, and the most effective moral force the world has ever known. We do not care, they say, whether the story of his birth, trial, death, and resur- rection is myth or actual history; such a man as Jesus may never have existed, the things he is reported as saying may have been put in his mouth by others, but what of that--is not the picture of his character perfect? Are not the Beatitudes beautiful- -no matter who said them? To strengthen this position they call our attention to Shakespeare's creations, the majority of whom--Hamlet, Othello, Lear, Portia, Imo- gen, Desdemona, are fictitious. Yet where are there grander men, or finer women? These children of Shakespeare may never have lived, but, surely, they will never die. In the same sense, Jesus may be just as ideal a character as those of Shakespeare, they say, and still be "the light of the world." A New York preacher is reported as saying that if Christianity is a lie, it is a "glorious lie."

My answer to the above is that such an argument evades instead of facing the question. It is receding from a position under cover of a rhetorical manoeuvre. It is a retreat in disguise. If Christianity is a "glorious lie," then call it such. The question under discussion is, Is Jesus Historical? To answer that it is immaterial whether or not he is historical, is to admit that there is no evidence that he is historical. To urge that, unhistorical though he be, he is, nevertheless, the only savior of the world, is, I regret to say, not only evasive,--not only does it beg the question, but it is also clearly dishonest. How long will the tremendous ecclesiastical machinery last, if it were candidly avowed that it is doubtful whether there ever was such a historical character as Jesus, or that in all probability he is no more real than one of Shakespeare's creations? What! all these prayers, these churches, these denominations, these sectarian wars which have shed oceans of human blood--these unfortunate persecutions which have blackened the face of man--the fear of hell and the devil which has blasted millions of lives--all these for a Christ who may, after all, be only a picture!

Neither is it true that this pictorial Jesus saved the world. He has had two thousand years to do it in, but as missionaries are still being sent out, it follows that the world is yet to be saved. The argument presented elsewhere in these pages may here be recapitulated.

There was war before Christianity; has Jesus abolished war?

There was poverty and misery in the world before Christianity; has Jesus removed these evils?

There was ignorance in the world before Christianity; has Jesus destroyed ignorance?

There were disease, crime, persecution, oppression, slavery, massacres, and bloodshed in the world before Christianity; alas, are they not still with us?

When Jesus shall succeed in pacifying his own disciples; in healing the sectarian world of its endless and bitter quarrels, then it will be time to ask what else Jesus has done for humanity.

If the world is improving at all, and we believe it is, the progress is due to the fact that man pays now more attention to *this* life than formerly. He is thinking less of the other world and more of this. He no longer sings with the believer:

> The world is all a fleeting show
>   For man's delusion given.
> Its smiles of joy, its tears of woe,
> Deceitful shine, deceitful flow,

There's nothing true but heaven.

How could people with such feelings labor to improve a world they hated? How could they be in the least interested in social or political reforms when they were constantly repeating to themselves--

I'm a pilgrim, and I'm a stranger--
I can tarry, I can tarry, but a night.

That these same people should now claim not only a part of the credit for the many improvements, but all of it--saying that, but for their religion the "world would now have been a hell," [Note: Rev. Frank Gunsaulus, of the Central Church, Chicago. See A New Catechism.--M. M. Mangasarian.] is really a little too much for even the most serene temperament.

Which of the religions has persecuted as long and as relentlessly as Christianity?

Which of the many faiths of the world has opposed Science as stubbornly and as bitterly as Christianity?

In the name of what other prophets have more people been burned at the stake than in the names of Jesus and Moses?

What other revelation has given rise to so many sects, hostile and irreconcilable, as the Christian?

Which religion has furnished as many effective texts for political oppression, polygamy, slavery, and the subjection of woman as the religion of Jesus and Paul?

Is there,--has there ever been another creed which makes salvation dependent on belief,--thereby encouraging hypocrisy, and making honest inquiry a crime?

To send a thief to heaven from the gallows because he believes, and an honest man to hell because he doubts, is that the virtue which is going to save the world?

The claim that Jesus has saved the world is another myth.

A *pictorial* Christ, then, has not done anything for humanity to deserve the tremendous expenditure of time, energy, love, and devotion, which has for two thousand years taxed the resources of civilization.

The passing away of this imaginary savior will relieve the world of an unproductive investment.

We conclude: Honesty, like charity, must begin at home. Unless we can tell the truth in our churches we will never tell the truth in our shops. Unless our teachers, the ministers of God, are honest, our insurance companies and corporations will have to be watched. Permit sham in your religious life, and the disease will spread to every member of the social body. If you may keep religion in the dark, and cry "hush," "hush," when people ask that it be brought out into the light, why may not politics or business cultivate a similar partiality for darkness? If the king cries, "rebel," when a citizen asks for justice, it is because he has heard the priest cry, "infidel," when a member of his church asked for evidence. Religious hypocrisy is the mother of all hypocrisies. Cure a man of that, and the human world will recover its health.

Not so long ago, nearly everybody believed in the existence of a personal devil. People saw him, heard him, described him, danced with him, and claimed, besides, to have whipped him. Luther hurled his inkstand at him, and American women accused as witches were put to death in the name of the devil. Yet all this "evidence" has not saved the devil from passing out of existence. What has happened to the devil will happen to the gods. Man is the only real savior. If he is not a savior, there is no other.

PART II.
IS THE WORLD INDEBTED TO CHRISTIANITY?

B ut," says the believer, again, as a last resort, "Jesus, whether real or mythical, has certainly saved the world, and is its only hope." If this assertion
can be supported with facts, then surely it would matter very little whether Jesus really lived and taught, or whether he is a mere picture. Although
even then it would be more truthful to say we have no satisfactory evidence that
such a teacher as Jesus ever lived, than to affirm dogmatically his existence, as it is
now done. Whatever Jesus may have done for the world, he has certainly not freed
us from the obligation of telling the truth. I call special attention to this point. Because Jesus has saved the world, granting for the moment that he has, is no reason
why we should be indifferent to the truth. Nay, it would show that Jesus has not
saved the world, if we can go on and speak of him as an actual existence, born of a
virgin and risen from the dead, and in his name persecute one another--oppose the
advance of science, deny freedom of thought, terrorize children and women with
pictures of hell-fire and seek to establish a spiritual monopoly in the world, when
the evidence in hand seems clearly to indicate that such a person never existed.

We shall quote a chapter from Christian history to give our readers an idea of
how much the religion of Jesus, when implicitly believed in, can do for the world.
We have gone to the earliest centuries for our examples of the influence exerted by
Christianity upon the ambitions and passions of human nature, because it is generally supposed that Christianity was then at its best. Let us, then, present a picture
of the world, strictly speaking, of the Roman Empire, during the first four or five
hundred years after its conversion to Christianity.

We select this specific period, because Christianity was at this time fifteen hundred years nearer to its source, and was more virile and aggressive than it has ever

been since.

Shakespeare speaks of the uses of adversity; but the uses of prosperity are even greater. The proverb says that "adversity tries a man." While there is considerable truth in this, the fact is that prosperity is a much surer criterion of character. It is impossible to tell, for instance, what a man will do who has neither the power nor the opportunity to do anything. "Opportunity," says a French writer, "is the cleverest devil." Both our good and bad qualities wait upon opportunity to show themselves. It is quite easy to be virtuous when the opportunity to do evil is lacking. Behind the prison bars, every criminal is a penitent, but the credit belongs to the iron bars and not to the criminal. To be good when one cannot be bad, is an indifferent virtue.

It is with institutions and religions as with individuals--they should be judged not by what they pretend in their weakness, but by what they do when they are strong. Christianity, Mohammedanism and Judaism, the three kindred religions-- we call them kindred because they are related in blood and are the offspring of the same soil and climate--these three kindred religions must be interpreted not by what they profess today, but by what they did when they had both the power and the opportunity to do as they wished.

When Christianity, or Mohammedanism, was professed only by a small handful of men--twelve fishermen, or a dozen camel-drivers of the desert--neither party advocated persecution. The worst punishment which either religion held out was a distant and a future punishment; but as soon as Christianity converted an Emperor, or Mohammed became the victorious warrior,--that is to say, as soon as, springing forth, they picked up the sword and felt their grip sure upon its hilt, this future and distant punishment materialized into a present and persistent persecution of their opponents. Is not that suggestive? Then, again, when in the course of human evolution, both Christianity and Mohammedanism lost the secular support--the throne, the favor of the courts, the imperial treasury--they fell back once more upon future penalties as the sole menace against an unbelieving world. As religion grows, secularly speaking, weaker, and is more completely divorced from the temporal, even the future penalties, from being both literal and frightful, pale into harmless figures of speech.

It was but a short time after the conversion of the Emperor Constantine, that the following edict was published throughout the provinces of the Roman Empire:

"O ye enemies of truth, authors and counsellors of death--we enact by this law that none of you dare hereafter to meet at your conventicles...nor keep any meetings either in public buildings or private houses. We have commanded that all your places of meeting--your temples--be pulled down or confiscated to the Catholic Church."

The man who affixed his signature to this edict was a monarch, that is to say, a man who had the power to do as he liked. The man and monarch, then, who affixed his imperial signature to this *first* document of persecution in Europe--the first, because, as Renan has beautifully remarked, "We may search in vain the whole Roman law before Constantine for a single passage against freedom of thought, and the history of the imperial government furnishes no instance of a prosecution for entertaining an abstract doctrine,"--this is glory enough for the civilization 'which we call *Pagan* and which was replaced by the Asiatic religion--the man and the monarch who fathered the first instrument of persecution in our Europe, who introduced into our midst the crazed hounds of religious wars, unknown either in Greece or Rome, Constantine, has been held up by Cardinal Newman as "a pattern to all succeeding monarchs." Only an Englishman, a European, infected with the malady of the East, could hold up the author of such an edict,--an edict which prostitutes the State to the service of a fad--as "a pattern."

If we asked for a modern illustration of what a church will do when it has the power, there is the example of Russia. Russia is today centuries behind the other European nations. She is the most unfortunate, the most ignorant, the most poverty-pinched country, with the most orthodox type of Christianity. What is the difference between Greek Christianity, such as prevails in Russia, and American Christianity! Only this: The Christian Church in Russia has both the power and the opportunity to do things, while the Christian church in America or in France has not. We must judge Christianity as a religion by what it does in Russia, more than by what it does not do in France or America. There was a time when the church did in France and in England what it is doing now in Russia, which is a further confirmation of the fact that a religion must be judged not by what it pretends in its weakness, but by what it does when it can. In Russia, the priest can tie a man's hands and feet and deliver him up to the government; and it does so. In Protestant countries, the church, being deprived of all its badges and prerogatives, is more modest and humble. The poet Heine gives eloquent expression to this idea when he says: "Religion comes begging to us, when it can no longer burn us."

There will be no revolution in Russia, nor even any radical improvement of existing conditions, so long as the Greek Church has the education of the masses in charge. To become politically free, men must first be intellectually emancipated. If a Russian is not permitted to choose his own religion, will he be permitted to choose his own form of government? If he will allow a priest to impose his religion upon him, why may he not permit the Czar to impose despotism upon him? If it is wrong for him to question the tenets of his religion, is it not equally wrong for him to discuss the laws of his government? If a slave of the church, why may he not be also a slave of the state? If there is room upon his neck for the yoke of the church, there will be room, also, for the yoke of the autocracy. If he is in the habit of bending his knees, what difference does it make to how many or to whom he bends them?

Not until Russia has become religiously emancipated, will she conquer political freedom. She must first cast out of her mind the fear of the church, before she can enter into the glorious fellowship of the free. In Turkey, all the misery of the people will not so much as cause a ripple of discontent, because the Moslem has been brought up to submit to the Sultan as to the shadow on earth of Allah. Both in Russia and Turkey, the protestants are the heretics. The orthodox Turk and the orthodox Christian permit without a murmur both the priest and the king to impose upon them at the point of a bayonet, the one his religion, and the other his government. It is only by taking the education of the masses out of the hands of the clergy that either country can enjoy any prosperity. Orthodoxy and autocracy are twins.

Let me now try to present to you a picture of the world under Christianity about the year 400 of the present era. Let us discuss this phase of the subject in a liberal spirit, extenuating nothing, nor setting down aught in malice. Please interpret what I say in the next few minutes metaphorically, and pardon me if my picture is a repellant one.

We are in the year of our Lord, 400:

I rose up early this morning to go to church. As I approached the building, I saw there a great multitude of people unable to secure admission into the edifice. The huge iron doors were closed, and upon them was affixed a notice from the authorities, to the effect that all who worshiped in this church would, by the authority of the state, be known and treated hereafter as "infamous heretics," and be exposed to the extreme penalty of the law if they persisted in holding services there. But the party to which I belonged heeded not the prohibition, but beat against the doors furiously and effected an entrance into the church. The excitement ran high; men and leaders shouted, gesticulated and came to blows. The Archbishop was urged to ascend his episcopal throne and officiate at the altar in spite of the formal interdiction against him. He consented. But he had not proceeded far when soldiers, with a wild rush, poured into the building and began to discharge arrows at the panic-stricken people. Instantly pandemonium was let loose. The officers commanding the soldiers demanded the head of the offending Archbishop. The worshipers made an attempt to resist; then blood was shed, the sight of which reeled people's heads, and, in an instant, the sanctuary was turned into a house of murder. Taking advantage of the uproar, the Archbishop, assisted by his secretaries, escaped through a secret door behind the altar.

On my way home from this terrible scene, I fell upon a procession of monks. They were carrying images and relics, and a banner upon which were inscribed these words: "The Virgin Mary, Mother of God." As they marched on, their number increased by new additions. But suddenly they encountered another band of monks, carrying a different banner, bearing the same words which were on the other party's banner, but instead of "The Virgin Mary, Mother of God," their banner read: "The Virgin Mary, Mother of Jesus Christ." The two processions clashed, and a bloody encounter followed; in an instant images, relics and banners were all in an indiscriminate heap. The troops were called out again, but such was the zeal of the conflicting parties that not until the majority of them were disabled and exhausted, was tranquility restored.

Looking about me, I saw the spire of a neighboring church. My curiosity prompted me to wend my steps thither. As soon as I entered, I was recognized as belonging to the forbidden sect, and in an instant a hundred fists rained down blows upon my head. "He has polluted the sanctuary," they cried. "He has committed sacrilege." "No quarter to the enemies of the true church," cried others, and it was a miracle that, beaten, bruised, my clothes torn from my back, I regained the street. A few seconds later, looking up the streets, I saw another troop of soldiers, rushing down toward this church at full speed. It seems that while I was being beaten in the main auditorium, in the baptistry of the church they were killing, in cold blood, the Archbishop, who was suspected of a predilection for the opposite party, and who had refused to retract or resign from his office. The next day I heard that one hundred and thirty-seven bodies were taken out of this building.

Seized with terror, I now began to run, but, alas, I had worse experiences in store for me. I was compelled to pass the principal square in the center of the city before I could reach a place of safety. When I reached this square, it had the appearance of a veritable battlefield. It was Sunday morning, and the partisans of rival bishops, differing in their interpretation of theological doctrines, were fighting each other like maddened, malignant creatures. One could hear, over the babel of discordant yells, scriptural phrases. The words, "The Son is equal to the Father," "The Father is greater than the Son," "He is begotten of the same substance as the Father," "He is of like substance, but not of the same substance," "You are a heretic," "You are an atheist," were invariably accompanied with blows, stabs and sword thrusts, until, as an eye- witness, I can take an oath that I saw the streets leading out of the square deluged with palpitating human blood. Suddenly the commander of the cavalry, Hermogenes, rode upon the scene of feud and bloodshed. He ordered the followers of the rival bishops to disperse, but instead of minding his authority, the zealots of both sides rushed upon his horse, tore the rider from the saddle and began to beat him with clubs and stones which they picked up from the street. He managed to escape into a house close by, but the religious rabble surrounded the house and set fire to it. Hermogenes appeared at the window, begging for his life. He was attacked again, and killed, and his mangled body dragged through the streets and rushed into a ditch.

The spectacle inflamed me, being a sectarian myself. I felt ashamed that I was not showing an equal zeal for *my* party. I, too, longed to fight, to kill, to be killed, for my religion. And, anon! the opportunity presented itself. I saw, looking up the street to my right, a group of my fellow-believers, who, like myself, shut out of their own church by the orthodox authorities, armed with whips loaded with lead and with clubs, were entering a house. I followed them. As we went in, we commanded the head of the family and his wife to appear. When they did, we asked them if it was true that in their prayers to Mary they had refrained from the use of the words,

"The mother of God." They hesitated to give a direct answer, whereupon we used the club, and then, the scourge. Then they said they believed in and revered the blessed virgin, but would not, even if we killed them, say that she was the mother of God. This obstinacy exasperated us and we felt it to be our religious duty, for the honor of our divine Queen, to perpetrate such cruelties upon them as would shock your gentle ears to hear. We held them over slowly burning fires, flung lime into their eyes, applied roasted eggs and hot irons to the sensitive parts of their bodies, and even gagged them to force the sacrament into their mouths.....As we went from house to house, bent upon our mission, I remember an expression of one of the party who said to the poor woman who was begging for mercy: "What! shall I be guilty of defrauding the vengeance of God of its victims?" A sudden chill ran down my back. I felt my flesh creep. Like a drop of poison the thought embodied in those words perverted whatever of pity or humanity was left in me, and I felt that I was only helping to secure victims with which to feed the vengeance of God!

I was willing to be a monster for the glory of God!

The Christian sect to which I belonged was one of the oldest in Christendom. Our ancestors were called the Puritans of the fourth and fifth centuries. We believe that no one can be saved outside of our communion. When a Christian of another church joins us, we re-baptize him, for we do not believe in the validity of other baptisms. We are so particular that we deny our cemeteries to any other Christians than our own members. If we find that we have, by mistake, buried a member of another church in our cemetery, we dig up his bones, that he may not pollute the soil. When one of the churches of another denomination falls into our hands, we first fumigate the building, and with a sharp knife we scrape the wood off the altars upon which other Christian priests have offered prayers. We will, under no consideration, allow a brother Christian from another church to commune with us; if by stealth anyone does, we spare not his life. But we are persecuted just as severely as we persecute, ourselves. [Note: This sect (Donatist) and others, lasted for a long time, and made Asia and Africa a hornet's nest,--a blood-stained arena, of feud and riot and massacre, until Mohammedanism put an end, in these parts of the world, not only to these sects, but to Christianity itself.]

As the sun was setting, fatigued with the holy Sabbath's religious duties, I started to go home. On my way back, I saw even wilder, bloodier scenes, between rival ecclesiastical factions, streets even redder with blood, if possible, yea, certain sections of the city seemed as if a storm of hail, or tongues of flame had swept over them. Churches were on fire, cowled monks attacking bishops' residences, rival prelates holding uproarious debates, which almost always terminated in bloodshed, and, to cap the day of many vicissitudes, I saw a bear on exhibition which had been given its freedom by the ruler, as a reward for his faithful services in devouring heretics. The Christian ruler kept two fierce bears by his own chamber, to which those who did not hold the orthodox faith were thrown in his presence while he listened with delight to their groans.

When I reached home, I was panting for breath. I had lived through another Sabbath day. [Note: If the reader will take the pains to read Dean Milman's History of Christianity, and his History of Latin Christianity; also Gibbon's Downfall of the Roman Empire, and Mosheim's History of Christianity, he will see that we have exaggerated nothing. The Athanasian and the Arian, the Donatist and Sabellian, the Nestorian and Alexandrian factions converted the early centuries into a long reign of terror.]

I feel like covering my face for telling you so grewsome a tale. But if this were the fourth or the fifth century, instead of the twentieth, and this were Constantinople, or Alexandria, or Antioch, instead of Chicago, I would have spent just such a Sunday as I have described to you. In giving you this concentrated view of human society in the great capitals of Christendom in the year 400, I have restrained, rather than spurred, my imagination. Remember, also, that I have confined my remarks to a specific and short period in history, and have excluded from my generalization all reference to the centuries of religious wars which tore Europe limb from limb,--the wholesale exterminations, the crusades, which represented one of the maddest spells of misguided and costly zeal which ever struck our earth, the persecution of the Huguenots, the extermination of the Albigenses and of the Waldenses,--the massacre of St. Bartholomew, the Inquisition with its red hand upon the intellect of Europe, the Anabaptist outrages in Germany, the Smithfield fires in England, the religious outrages in Scotland, the Puritan excesses in America,--the reign of witchcraft and superstition throughout the twenty centuries--I have not touched my picture with any colors borrowed from these terrible chapters in the history of our unfortunate earth. I have also left out all reference to Papal Rome, with its dungeons, its stakes, its massacres and its burnings. I have said nothing of Galileo, Vanini, Campanella or Bruno. I have passed over all this in silence. You can imagine, now, how much more repellant and appalling this representation of the Roman world under Christianity would have been had I stretched my canvas to include also these later centuries.

But I tremble to be one-sided or unjust, and so I hasten to say that during the twenty centuries' reign of our religion, the world has also seen some of the fairest flowers spring out of the soil of our earth. During the past twenty centuries there have been men and women, calling themselves Christians, who have been as generous, as heroic and as deeply consecrated to high ideals as any the world has ever produced. Christianity has, in many instances, softened the manners of barbarians and elevated the moral tone of primitive peoples. It gives us more pleasure to speak of the good which religions have accomplished than to call attention to the evil they have caused. But this raises a very important question. "Why do you not confine yourself," we are often asked, "to the virtues you find in Christianity or Mohammedanism, instead of discussing so frequently their short-comings? Is it not better to praise than to blame, to recommend than to find fault?" This is a fair question, and we may just as well meet it now as at any other time.

Such is the economy of nature that no man, or institution or religion, can be altogether evil. The poet spoke the truth when he said: "There is a soul of goodness in things evil." Evil, in a large sense, is the raw material of the good. All things contribute to the education of man. The question, then, whether an institution is helpful or hurtful, is a relative one. The character of an institution, as that of an individual, is determined by its ruling passion. Despotism, for instance, is generally considered to be an evil. And yet, a hundred good things can be said of despotism. The French people, over a hundred years ago, overthrew the monarchy. And yet the monarchy had rendered a thousand services to France. It was the monarchy that created France, that extended her territory, developed her commerce, built her great cities, defended her frontiers against foreign invasion, and gave her a place among the first-class nations of Europe. Was it just, then, to pull down an institution that had done so much for France?

Why did the Americans overthrow British rule in this country? Had not England rendered innumerable services to the colony? Was she not one of the most progressive, most civilizing influences in the modern world? Was it just, then, that we should have beaten out of the land a government that had performed for us so many friendly acts?

Referring once more to the case of Russia: Why do the awakened people in that country demand the overthrow of the autocracy? Is there nothing good to be said of Russian autocracy? Have not the Czars loved their country and fought for her prosperity? Have they not brought Russia up to her present size, population and political influence in Europe? Have they not beautified her cities and enacted laws for the protection of their subjects? Is it right, then, in spite of all these things that autocracy has done for Russia, to seek to overthrow it?

Once more: Why do the missionaries go into India and China and Japan trying to replace the ancestral religion of these people with the Christian faith? Why does the missionary labor to overthrow the worship of Buddha, Confucius and Zoroaster? Have not these great teachers helped humanity? Have they not rendered any services to their countrymen? Are there no truths in their teachings? Are there no virtues in their lives? Is it right, then, that the missionary should criticise these ancient faiths?

Let us take an example from nearer home. We were talking some years ago with a gentleman who had just returned from Dowie's Zion. He was surprised to find there a clean, orderly and well-behaved people, apparently quite happy. He said that after his experiences there, he would rather do business with Dowie and his men than with the average member of other religious bodies. He found the Dowieites honest, reliable and peaceful. Now, all this may be true, and I hope it is; but what of it? Dowieism is an evil, notwithstanding this recital of its virtues. It is an evil, because it arrests the intellectual development of man, because it makes dwarfs of the people it converts, because it pinches the forehead of each convert into that of either a charlatan or an idiot. We regret to have to use these harsh terms. But Dowieism is denounced, because it brings up human beings as if they were sheep, because it robs them of the most glorious gift of life, the freedom to grow, Dowieism is an evil, because it makes the human race mediocre by contracting its intellect down to the measure of a creed. We would much rather that the Dowieites smoked and drank and swore, than that they should fear to think. There is hope for a bad man. There is no hope for the stupid.

In the case of an institution or a religion, then, it is not by adding up the debit and credit columns and striking a balance sheet that the question whether it has helped or hurt mankind is to be determined. We cannot, for instance, place ninety-nine vices in one column, and a hundred virtues in another, and conclude therefrom that the institution or the religion should be preserved. Nor, conversely speaking, can we place a hundred vices against ninety-nine virtues, and, therefore, condemn, the institution. Even as a man is hanged for one act in his life, in spite of the thousand good acts which may be quoted against the one evil deed, so an institution or a religion is honored or condemned, as we said above, for its *ruling passion*. Mohammedanism, Judaism and Christianity have done much good, just as other religions have, but they are condemned today by modern thought, because they are a conspiracy against reason--because they combat progress, as if it were a crime!

Another criticism frequently advanced against us is that we fail to realize that all the evil of which Christianity is said to have been the cause, is only the result of human ignorance and passion. When attention is called, for instance, to the intolerance and stubborn opposition to science, of Christianity, the answer given is, that this conduct is not only not inspired by the spirit of Christianity, but that it is in direct contradiction to its teachings. The Christians claim that all the luminous chapters in history have been inspired by their religion, all its sorrowful and black pages have been written by the passions of men. But this apology, which, we regret to say, is in every preacher's mouth, is not an honest one. In our opinion, both Mohammedanism and Christianity, as also Judaism, are responsible for the evil as well as the good they have accomplished in the world. They are responsible for the lives they have destroyed, as for the lives they have saved. They are responsible for the passions they have aroused,--for the hatred, the persecutions and the religious wars of the centuries, as for the piety and charity they have encouraged.

The central idea in all the three religions mentioned above, is that God has revealed his will to man. There is, we say frankly, the root of all the evil which religion has inflicted upon our unfortunate earth. The poison is in both the flower and the fruit which that idea brings forth. If it be true that God has revealed his will, that he has told us, for instance, to believe in the Trinity, the atonement, the fall of man, and the dogma of eternal punishment, and we refuse to do so, will we not, then, be regarded as the most odious, the most heinous, the most rebellious, the most sacrilegious, the most stiff- necked, the most criminal people in the world? Think of refusing to believe as God has dictated to us! Think of saying *no!* to one's Creator and Father in Heaven! Think of the consequences of differing with God, and tempting others to do the same! Is it at all strange that during the early centuries of Christianity, the people who hesitated to agree with the deity, or to believe as he wanted them to, were looked upon as incarnate fiends, as the accomplices of the devil and the enemies of the human race, and were treated accordingly?

The doctrine of salvation by faith makes persecution inevitable. If to refuse to believe in the Trinity, or in the divinity of Christ, is a crime against God and will be punished by an eternity of hell in the next world, and if such a man endangers the eternal salvation of his fellows, is it not the duty of all religious people to endeavor to exterminate him and his race, now arid here? How can Christian people tolerate the rebel against their God, when God himself has pronounced sentence of death against him? Why not follow the example of the deity, as set forth in the persecutions of the Old Testament?

When we have a God for a teacher, the highest and surest virtue is unconditional acquiescence. Judaism, Mohammedanism and Christianity, in giving us a God for a teacher, have taken away from us the liberty to think for ourselves. Each one of these three religions makes unconditional obedience the price of the salvation it offers, but do you know what other word in the English language unconditional obedience is a synonym of?--Silence! A dumb world, a tongue-tied humanity alone can be saved! The good man is the man on his knees with his mouth in the dust. But silence is sterility! Silence is slavery! Think, then, of the character of a religion which makes free speech, free thought, a crime--which hurls hell against the Protestant!

There is a third question to be answered: It is true, they say to us, that there are many things in the Koran, the Old Testament and the New, which are really injurious, and which ought to be discarded, but there are also many beautiful principles, noble sentiments and high educational maxims in these scriptures. Why not, then, dwell upon these, and pass in silence over the objectionable teachings of these religions? It is not necessary to repeat again that in all so-called sacred scriptures, there are glorious truths. It could not have been otherwise. All literature, whether secular or religious, is the voice of man and sweeps the whole compass of human love and hope. We have no objection to quoting from the Veddas, the Avestas, the Koran or the Bible; nor do we hesitate to admire and enjoy and praise generously the ravishingly beautiful utterances of the poets and prophets of all times and climes. Nevertheless, it remains true that the modern world finds more practical help and inspiration in secular authors, in the books of science and philosophy, than in these so-called inspired scriptures. Jesus, who is popularly believed to have preached the Sermon on the Mount, has said little or nothing which can help the modern world as much as the scientific revelations of a student like Darwin, or of a philosopher like Herbert Spencer, or of a poet like Goethe or Shakespeare. We know this will sound like blasphemy to the believer, but a moment's honest and fearless reflection will convince everyone of the fact that neither Mohammed nor Jesus had in view modern conditions when they delivered their sermons. Jesus could have had no idea of a world outside of his little Palestine. The thought of the many races of the world mingling together in one country could never have occurred to him. His vision did not embrace the vista of two thousand years, nor did his mind rise to the level of the problems which today tax the brain and heart of man. Jesus believed implicitly that the world would speedily come to an end, that the sun and the moon would soon fall from the face of the sky, and that people living then in Palestine would not taste of death before they saw "the Son of Man return upon the clouds." Jesus had no idea of a progressive evolution of humanity. It was beyond him to conceive the consolidation of the nations into one fellowship, the new resources which science would tap, or the new energies which human industry would challenge. Jesus was in peaceful ignorance of the social and international problems which confront the world of today. The Sermon on the Mount, then, which is said to be the best in our gospels, can be of little help to us, for it could not have been meant for us. And it is very easy to show that the modern world ignores, not out of disrespect to Jesus, but by the force of circumstances and the evolution of society, the principles contained in that renowned sermon.

I was waiting for transportation at the corner of one of the principal streets of Chicago, the other day, when, looking about me, I saw the tremendous buildings which commerce and wealth have reared in our midst. On one hand was a savings bank, on the other a colossal national bank, and up and down the street a thousand equally solid and substantial buildings, devoted to the interests of commerce and civilization. To bring out and emphasize the wide breach between the man who preached the Sermon on the Mount, and progressive and aggressive, busy and wealthy, modern Chicago, I took the words of Jesus and mentally inscribed them upon the walls of these buildings. Upon the savings bank--and a savings bank represents economy, frugality, self-sacrifice, self-restraint,--the desire of the people to provide for the uncertainties of the future, to lay by something for the education of their children, for the maintenance of their families when they themselves have ceased to live,--I printed upon the facade of this institution, figuratively speaking, these words of the Oriental Jesus:

"Take no thought of the morrow, for the morrow will take care of itself."

And upon the imposing front of the national bank, I wrote: "Lay not up for yourselves treasures on earth." If we followed these teachings, would not our industrial and social life sink at once to the level of the stagnating Asiatics?

Pursuing this comparison between Jesus and modern life, I inscribed upon the handsome churches whose pews bring enormous incomes, and on the palatial residences of Bishops, with salaries of from twenty-five to a hundred thousand dollars, these words:

"How hardly shall a rich man enter into the kingdom of Heaven," and, "It is easier for a camel to go through the eye of a needle than for a rich man to enter the kingdom of Heaven."

In plain words, the gospel condemns wealth, and cries, "Woe unto you rich," and "Sell all thou hast and give it to the poor," which, by the way, would only be shifting the temptation of wealth from one class to another. Buckle was nearer the truth, and more modern in spirit, when he ascribed the progress of man to the pursuit of truth and the acquisition of wealth.

But let us apply the teachings of Jesus to still other phases of modern life. Some years ago our Cuban neighbors appealed to the United States for protection against the cruelty and tyranny of Spanish rule. We sent soldiers over to aid the oppressed and down-trodden people in the Island. Now, suppose, instead of sending iron-clads and admirals,--Schley, Sampson and Dewey,--we had advised the Cubans to "resist not evil," and to "*submit* to the powers that be," or suppose the General of our army, or the Secretary of our navy, had counseled seriously our soldiers to remember the words of Jesus when fighting the Spaniards: "If a man smite thee on one cheek," etc. Write upon our halls of justice and courthouses and statute books, and on every lawyer's desk, these solemn words of Jesus: "He that taketh away thy coat, let him have thy cloak also."

Introduce into our Constitution, the pride and bulwark of our liberties, guaranteeing religious freedom unto all,--these words of Paul: "If any man preach any other gospel than that which I have preached unto you, let him be accursed." Think of placing nearly fifty millions of our American population under a curse!

Tell this to the workers in organized charities: "Give to every man that asketh of thee," which, if followed, would make a science of charity impossible.

To the workingmen, or the oppressed seeking redress and protesting against evil, tell this: "Blessed are they that are persecuted," which is equivalent to encouraging them to submit to, rather than to resist, oppression.

Or upon our colleges and universities, our libraries and laboratories consecrated to science, write the words: "The wisdom of this world is foolishness with God," and "God has chosen the foolish to confound the wise."

Ah, yes, the foolish of Asia, it is true, succeeded in confounding the philosophers of Europe. Abraham, Isaac, Jacob, Moses, Jesus, did replace Socrates, Plato, Aristotle, Seneca, Cicero, Caesar and the Antonines! But it was a trance, a spell, a delirium only, and it did not last,--it could not last. The charm is at last broken. Europe is forever free from the exorcism of Asia.

I believe the health and sanity and virtue of our Europe would increase a hundred fold, if we could, from this day forth, cease to pretend professing by word of mouth what in our own hearts and lives we have completely outgrown. If we could be sincere and brave; if our leaders and teachers would only be honest with themselves and honest with the modern world, there would, indeed, be a new earth and a new humanity.

But the past is past. It is for us to sow the seeds which in the day of their fruition shall emancipate humanity from the pressing yoke of a stubborn Asiatic superstition, and push the future even beyond the beauty and liberty of the old Pagan world!

CHRISTIANITY AND PAGANISM

Christianity as an Asiatic cult is not suitable to European races. To prove this, let us make a careful comparison between Paganism and Christianity. There are many foolish things, and many excellent things, in both the Pagan and the Christian religions. We are not concerned with particular beliefs and rites; it is Paganism as a philosophy of life, and Christianity as a philosophy of life, that we desire to investigate. And at the threshold of our investigation we must bear in mind that Paganism was born and grew into maturity in Europe, while Asia was the cradle of Christianity. It would be superfluous to undertake to prove that in politics, in government, in literature, in art, in science, in the general culture of the people, Europe was always in advance of Asia.

Do we know of any good reason, when it comes to religion, why Asia should be incomparably superior to anything Europe has produced in that line? Unless we believe in miracles, the natural inference would be that a people who were better educated in every way than the Asiatics should have also possessed the better religion. I admit that this is only inferential, or *a priori* reasoning, and that it still remains to be shown by the recital of facts, that Europe not only ought to have produced a better religion than Asia, but that she did.

In my opinion, between the Pagan and Christian view of life there is the same difference that there is between a European and an Asiatic. What makes a Roman a Roman, a Greek a Greek, and a Persian a Persian? That is a very interesting, but also a very difficult question. Why are not all nations alike? Why is the oak more robust than the spruce? What are the subtle influences which operate in the womb of nature, where "the embryos of races are nourished into form and individuality?" I cannot answer that question satisfactorily, and I am not going to attempt to answer it at all. We know there is a radical difference between the European and the Asiatic; we know that Oriental and Occidental culture are the antitheses of each other, and nowhere else is this seen more clearly than in their interpretations of the universe, that is to say, in their religions.

In order to understand the Oriental races, we must discover the standpoint from which they take their observations.

But first, it is admitted, of course, that there are Europeans who are more Asiatic in their habits of life and thought than the Asiatics themselves, and, conversely, there are Asiatics who in spirit, energy and progressiveness are abreast of the most advanced representatives of European culture.

Nor has Asia been altogether barren; she has blossomed in many spots, and she nursed the flame of civilization at a time when Europe was not yet even cradled.

To show the intellectual point of view of the Asiatic, let me quote a passage from the Book of Job, which certainly is an Oriental composition, and one of the finest:

"How, then, can man be justified with God, or how can he be clean that is born of a woman? *Man that is a worm, and the son of man, which is a worm*."

This, then, is the standpoint of the Oriental. He believes he is a poor little worm. His philosophy must necessarily *trail* in the dust. A worm cannot have the thoughts of an eagle; a worm cannot have the imagination of a *Titan*; a worm sees the world only as a worm may. This is the angle of vision of the Asiatic. He calls himself a worm, and naturally his view of life shrinks to the limits of his standpoint. To he perfectly fair, however, we must admit there are passages in all the bibles of the Orient which are as daring as those found in any European book, but they represent only the strayings of the Oriental mind, not its normal pulse. The habitual accent of the Oriental is that man, calling a woman his mother, is a worm. In the Psalms of David, or whoever wrote the book, we read these words: "*I am a worm, and not a man*." What did the Oriental see in the worm, which induced him to select it out of all things as the original, so to speak, of man? The worm *crawls* and *creeps* and *writhes*. Nothing is so distressing as to see its helpless wiggling--and its home is in the dust; dirt is its daily food. Moreover, it is in danger of being stamped or trampled into annihilation at any instant. A worm *represents the minimum* of worth,--the dregs in the cup of existence; it is the scum or the froth of life, which one may blow into the air. It is impossible to descend lower than this in self-abasement.

When the Oriental, therefore, says that man is a worm or "I am a worm," he is just as much *obeying the cumulative* pressure of his Asiatic ancestry, and voicing the inherited submission of the Oriental mind, as Prometheus, with the vulture at his breast, and shaking his hand in the face of the gods, expresses the revolt of the European mind. The normal state for the Asiatic is submission; for the European it is independence. Slavery has a fascination for the children of the east. The air of independence is too sharp for them. They crave a master, a Sultan or a Czar, who shall own them body and soul. Through long practice, they have acquired the art of servility and flattery, of salaams and prostrations--an art in which they have become so efficient that it would be to them like throwing away so much capital to abandon its practice. They expect to go to Heaven on their knees. This is not said to hurt the feelings of the races of the Orient. We are explaining the influence of absolutism upon the products and tendencies of the human mind. The religion of the Orient, then, notwithstanding its many beautiful features like its politics, is a ***product of the suppressed*** mind, which finds in the creeping worm of the dust the measure of its own worth. How different is the European from the Asiatic in this respect! The latter crawls upon the stage of this magnificent universe with the timidity, hesitancy and tremblings of a worm. True to his bringing up, he falls prostrate, overwhelmed by the marvelous immensities opening before him and the abysses yawning at his feet. He contracts and dwindles in size, imploring with outstretched hands to be spared because he is a poor worm. It is a part of his religion or philosophy that if he admits he is nothing but a worm, the dread powers will not consider him a rival or a rebel, but will look upon him as a confirmed subject, and permit him to live. This is his art, the strategy by which he hopes to secure his salvation.

There has never been a republic in Asia, which is another way of saying that the Asiatic mind has never asserted its independence. Hence its thought smacks of slavery. In politics, as in religion, the Asiatic has always been passive. He has never been an actor, but only a spectator. It is his to nod the head, fold the arms and bend the knee. On earth he must have a king and a pope, and in heaven an Allah or a Jehovah. He has not been created for himself, but for the glory of his earthly and heavenly Lords. This radical difference between European self-appreciation and Asiatic self-depreciation furnishes the key to the problem under discussion.

Paganism is the religion of a self-governing race. Buddhism, Judaism, Mohammedanism, and Christianity are religions born on a soil where man is owned by another. It will be impossible to imagine Marcus Aurelius, for instance, crawling upon his knees before any being, or calling himself a worm. One must have in his blood the taint of a thousand years of slavery, before he can stoop so low. Marcus Aurelius was a gentleman. The European conception of a gentleman implies self-respect and independence; the Oriental conception of a gentleman implies self- abasement and acquiescence. The Oriental gentleman is a man who serves his king as though he were his slave.

But observe now how the Oriental proceeds to pull down his mind to the level of his body, which he has likened to a worm. When I was still a Presbyterian minister, I was invited to address a Sunday-school camp- meeting at Asbury Park in New Jersey. There were other speakers besides myself; one of them, known as a Sunday-school leader, had brought with him a chart of the human heart, which, when he arose to address the children, he spread on a blackboard before them: "This is a picture of your heart before you have accepted Jesus. What do you think of it?" he asked the school. "It is all black," was the answer; and it was. He had drawn a totally black picture to represent the heart of the child before conversion.

In all the literature of Pagandom, there is not the least intimation of so fearful an idea as the total depravity of human nature. The Pagans never thought, spoke, or heard of such a thing. It was inconceivable to them; they would have recoiled from it as from a species of barbarism. How radically different, then, must European culture have been from the Asiatic. There is a gulf well-nigh impassible between the thought of a free-born citizen and that of the oppressed and enslaved Oriental.

But let us continue. Not satisfied with thinking of himself as a worm, and of his intellectual and moral nature as totally degraded, the Oriental strikes with the same paralyzing stroke, at ***the world in which he lives***, until it, too, withers and becomes an ugly and heinous thing. He calls the world a "vale of tears," ruled by the powers of darkness, and groaning under a primeval curse. "The world, the flesh and the devil" become a trio of iniquity and sin. Some of you in your earlier days must have sung that Methodist hymn which represents the world as a snare and a delusion:

> "The world is a fleeting show
> For man's illusion given."

Given! Think of believing that the world has been purposely given us to lead us astray. The thought staggers the mind. It suggests a terrible conspiracy against man. For his ruin, sun, moon and stars co- operate with the devil. Help! we cry, as we realize our inability to cope with the tremendous powers hurling themselves against us like billows of the raging sea, and taking our breath away. It suggests that we are placed in a world which has been made purposely beautiful, in order to tempt us into sin. Think of such a belief! It is that of a slave. It is Asiatic; it is not European. Neither you nor I, in all our readings, have ever come across any such attitude toward nature in Pagan literature. The Greeks and the Romans loved nature and made lovely gods out of. every running brook, caressing zephyr, dancing wave, glistening dew, sailing cloud, beaming star, beautiful woman, or brave man. The Oriental suspects nature and regards her smiles--the shining of the sun, the perfume of the meadows, the swell of the sea, the fluttering of the branches tipped with blossoms, the emerald grass, the sapphire sky--looks upon all these as the seductive advances of a prostitute in whose embrace lurks death!

But, once more; not satisfied with dragging the world down to the plane of his totally depraved nature, and that again to the level of the worm, the Asiatic projects his fatal thought into the next world and, crossing the grave, that silent and painless home of a tired race, he crowds the beyond with a thousand thousand pains and aches and horrors and fires--with sulphur and brimstone and burning hells. His frightened imagination invokes dark and infernal beings without number, fanning with their dark wings the very air he breathes. This is too revolting to think of. Poor slave! Inured to suffering,--to the lash, to oppression's crushing heel,--he dare not dream of a painless future, of a quiet, peaceful sleep at life's end, nor has he the divine audacity to invent a new world wherein the misery and slavery of his present existence will be impossible,--where all his tyrants will be dead, where he shall taste of sweet freedom and become himself a god. In his timidity and shrinking submission, with the spring of his heart broken, his spirit crushed, all independence strangled in his soul,--he puts in the biggest corner of his heaven even,--a *hell*!

Nor does he pause there, but, stinging his slave imagination once more, he declares that this future of torture and hell-fire is *everlasting*. He cannot improve upon that. Deeper in degradation he cannot descend. That is the darkest thought he can have, and, strange to say, he hugs it to his bosom as a mother would her child. The doctrine of hell is the thought of a slave and of a coward. No free-horn man, no brave soul could ever have invented so abhorrent an idea. Only under a regime of absolutism, only under an Oriental Sultan whose caprice is law, whose vengeance is terrible, whose favors are fickle, whose power is crushing, whose greed is insatiable, whose torture instruments are without number, and whose dark dungeons always resound with the rattling of chains and the groans of martyrs--only under such a regime could man have invented an unending hell. But we were mistaken when we said that hell was the darkest that the Asiatic was capable of. He has grafted upon the European mind a belief which is darker still.

Is there anything more precious in human life than children? The sternest heart melts, the fiercest features relax, at the sight of an innocent, sweet, laughing, frolicking babe in its mother's arms. Look at its glorious eyes, so full of surprises, so deep, so appealing! Look at the soft round hands, the little feet, the exquisite mouth, opening like a bud! Hear its prattle, which is nothing but the mind beginning to stir! Watch its gestures, the first language of the child! See it with its tiny arms about its mother's neck. Mark its joy when it is kissed. What else in our human world is more beautiful, more divine? And yet, and yet, the slave creed of Asia has drawn into its burning net of damnation even the cradle. John Burroughs describes how in a Catholic cemetery near where he lives he was shown a neglected, unkept corner, used for the burial of unbaptized children. Consecrated ground is denied to them, and so their poor bodies are huddled together in this profane plot, unblessed and unsaved. I do not wish to live in a world where such absurdities are not only coun- tenanced, but where they are exalted even to the dignity of a religion!

O holy children! O sweet children! huddled together in unconsecrated ground, and thus exposed to the cruelty of indescribable demons! Can you hear me? I am a man of compassion. I can forgive the murderer. I can pardon and pity the meanest wretch and take him into my arms, but I confess that even if I had a heart as big as the ocean, I could not, I would not, forgive the creed that can be guilty of such inhumanity against you,--dear, innocent ones, who were born to breathe but for a moment the harsh air of this world! When such gloom overpowers me and wrings from my lips such hard words, I find some little respite in contemplating the old Pagan world in its best days. I hasten for consolation to my Pagan friends, and in their sanity find healing for my bruised heart.

In one of his letters, the Greek Plutarch says this about children, which I want you to compare with what St. Augustine, the representative of the Asiatic creed, says on the same subject. "It is irreligious," writes Plutarch, "to lament for those pure souls (the children) who have passed into a better life and a happier dwelling place." [Note: Plutarch Ad Uxorem. Comp. Lecky's History of European Morals. Vol. I.] Compare this Pagan tenderness for children with the Asiatic doctrine of infant damnation but recently thrown out of the Presbyterian creed. Yet, if St. Augustine is to be believed, it is a heresy to reject the damnation of unbaptized infants: "Whosoever shall tell," writes this Father of the church, "that infants shall be quickened in Christ who died without partaking in his sacrament, does both contradict the apostles' teaching and condemn the whole church." [Note: St. Augustine Epist. 166.] It is infinitely more religious to disagree with the apostles and the church, if that is their teaching. The Pagan view of children is the holier view. The doctrine of the damnation of children could only find lodgment in the brain of a slave or a madman. It is Asiatic and altogether foreign to the culture of Europe.

All that we have advanced thus far may be summed up in one phrase: Asia invented the idea that man is a ***fallen*** being. This idea, which is the ***dors espinal***,--the backbone--of Christianity, never for once entered the mind of the European. We have already quoted from Job and the Psalms; the following is from the book of Jeremiah: "The heart is deceitful above all things and desperately wicked." This is one of the texts upon which the doctrine of the fall of man is based. We repeat that only under a religion of slavery, where one slave vies with another to abase himself before his lords and masters, could such an idea have been invented. There is not a man in all our sacred scriptures who could stand before the deity erect and unabashed, or who could speak in the accents of a Cicero who said, "We boast justly of our own virtue, which we could not do if we derived it from the deity and not from ourselves," or this from Epictetus, "It is characteristic of a wise man that he looks for all his good and evil from himself." Such independence was foreign to a race that believed itself ***fallen***.

In further confirmation of our position, it may be said that the models which the Pagans set up for emulation were men like themselves, only nobler. The models which the Orientals set up for imitation, on the other hand, were supernatural beings, or men who were supposed to possess supernatural powers. The great men for the Oriental are men who can work miracles, who possess magical powers, who possess secrets and can know how to influence the deity,--Moses, Joshua, David, Joseph, Isaiah, Jesus, Paul,--all demi-divinities. The Pagans, on the other hand, selected natural men, men like themselves, who had earned the admiration of their fellows. Let me quote to you Plutarch's eloquent sentence relative to this subject: "Whenever we begin an enterprise or take possession of a charge, or experience a calamity, we place before our eyes the examples of the greatest men of our own or of bygone ages, and we ask ourselves how Plato, or Epaminondas, or Lycurgus, or Agesilaus, would have acted. Looking into these personages, as into a faithful mirror, we can remedy our defects in word or deed."

The Westminster Catechism, which in its essentials is a resume of our Asiatic religion, emphasizes the doctrine of the fall of man, of which the Pagan world knew nothing, and refused to believe it until priests succeeded in dominating the mind of Europe: "The catechism following the Scripture teaches that...we are not only a disinherited family, but we are personally depraved and demoralized." [Note: Westminster Catechism, Comments.] Goodness! the Oriental imagination, abused by slavery, cannot rid itself of the idea of being disinherited, turned out into the cold, orphaned and smitten with moral sores from head to foot. To the Pagan, such a description of man would have been the acme of absurdity. Again: "It (the fall) affirms that he (man) is all wrong, in all things and all the time." [Note: Westminster Catechism, Comments.] If this was comforting news to the Asiatic, the Pagan world would have rejected the idea as unworthy of men in their senses. Once more: "All mankind by their fall lost communion with God, are under his wrath and curse, and so made liable to all miseries in this life and to the pains of hell forever." [Note: Westminster Catechism, Comments.] And this is the Gospel we have imported from Asia!

Is it not pathetic? Could slavery ever strike a deeper bottom than that? Standing before his owner, the Asiatic, of his own choice, hands himself over to be degraded, to be placed in chains and delivered up to the torments of hell forever. I despair of man. I would cry my heart out if I permitted myself to dwell upon the folly and stupidity and slavery of which man voluntarily makes himself the victim. Think of it! A man and a woman, nobody knows where or when, are supposed to have tasted of the fruit of a tree; the Oriental mind, with its crouching imagination, pounces upon this flimsy, fanciful tale with the appetite of a carrion crow, and exalts it to the dignity of an excuse for the eternal damnation of a whole world. I am dazed! I can say no more!

Let us recapitulate. The Oriental distrust of the natural man, born of self-depreciation, which is the fruit of prolonged slavery, develops into a sort of mental canker spreading at a raging pace until the whole universe, with its glorious sun and stars, becomes an object of horror and loathing. Not satisfied with thinking of himself as a worm, of his intellectual and moral nature as totally depraved, he communicates his disease to the world in which he lives until it, too, shrinks and wastes away. Then the disease, finding no more on this side of the grave to feed upon, leaps over the grave and converts the beyond, the virgin worlds, into an *inferno* with which to satiate its fear. Indeed frightful are the thoughts of a slave people!

Let me now, in conclusion, call your attention to another difference between the Occidental and the Oriental mind. When the body is feeble or ill-nourished, it is less liable to resist disease; likewise when the mind is alarmed, cowed, or pinched with fear, it becomes more exposed to superstition. Superstition is the disease of the mind. It will keep away from robust minds, as physical disease from a body in health. Now, the Asiatic mind, scared into silence and subjection,--starved to a mere shadow of what it should be, falls an easy prey to all the maladies that mind is heir to. The European mind, on the other hand, with room and air to move and grow in, develops a vitality which offers resistance to all attacks of mental disease. That explains why superstition thrives with ignorance and slavery, and expires when science and liberty gain the ascendency. Sanitary precautions prevent physical disease; knowledge and liberty constitute the therapeutics of the mind. Why is the Oriental so prone or partial to miracle and mystery? His mind is sick. To believe is easier to him than to reason. He follows the line of the least resistance: he has invented faith that he may not have to think. The mental cells in his brain are so starved, so devitalized, that they have to be whipped into movement. Only the bizarre, the monstrous, the supernatural,--demons, ghosts, dream worlds, miracles and mysteries,--can hold his attention. Not science, but metaphysics, barren speculation,--is the product of the Oriental mind. The philosopher Bacon describes the Asiatic when he speaks of men who "have hitherto dwelt but little, or rather only slightly touched upon experience, whilst they have wasted much time on theories and fictions of the imagination."

Again: I sometimes think that if it be true that monotheism, the idea of one God, was first discovered in Asia, it must have been suggested to them by the regime of Absolutism, under which they lived. Unlike Asia, democratic Europe believed in a republic of gods. Polytheism is more consonant with the republican idea, than monotheism. If we would let the American President rule the land without the aid of the two houses of congress or his cabinet ministers, his power would be infinitely more than it is now, but his gain would be the people's loss. His increased power would only represent so much more power taken away from the people. One God means not only more slaves, but more abject, more helpless ones. One God is a centralization which reduces man's liberty to a minimum. With more gods, and gods at times disagreeing among themselves, and all bidding for man's support, man would count for more. The Greeks could not tolerate a Jehovah, or an Allah, before whom the Oriental rabble bent the knee. "Allah knows," exclaims the Moslem; that is why the Mohammedans continue in ignorance. "Allah is great," cries again the Turk. That is why he himself is small. The more powerful the sovereign, the smaller the subject.

Now this leads us to a final reflection upon the difference between the mind brought up under restraint,--in slavery,--and the mind of the free. "The Pagan," to quote Lecky, "believed that to become acceptable to the deity, one must be virtuous;" the Asiatic doctrine, on the contrary, taught that "the most heroic efforts of human virtue are insufficient to avert a sentence of eternal condemnation, unless united with an implicit belief" in the dogmas of religion. In other words, the noblest of men cannot be saved by his own merits of character alone, for even when we have done our best, we are but "unprofitable slaves," quoting a Bible text. Only by the merits of Christ, or by the grace of God, can any man be saved. Have you ever paused to think of the purport of this piece of Orientalism? It wipes out every imaginable claim or right of man. Even when he is just and great and good, he has no rights, he is as vile as the vilest. Only the favor of the king can save,--only the grace of God, who can save the thief on the cross if he so pleases. Is he not absolute? If he extends his scepter, you live; if he smiles you are spared; if he patronizes you, you are fortunate. He says, live! you live. He says, die! you die. This is the apotheosis of despotism exalted into a revelation.

What, then, is our creed, but the thoughts of an eastern slave population, cringing before the throne of a Sultan, and one by one signing away their liberties? "The foundation of all real grandeur is a spirit of proud and lofty independence," says Buckle; but that is not the spirit of Asia, or of its religion. It is, and we ought to try to keep it, the spirit of the Western world.

I cannot imagine how we in this country, born of sturdy parents, born of the freedom-loving Pagans of Rome and Greece, born of men who shook their hands in the face of heaven, and pulled the gods off their thrones when they violated the rights of man,--I cannot understand how we have thrown overboard the proud, lofty spirit of independence of the Pagans,--our forefathers, and taken upon our necks the strangling yoke of the slave-thought of Asia!

PART III.
SOME MODERN OPINIONS ABOUT JESUS.

Christianity "dwells with noxious exaggeration about the person of Jesus."--Emerson.

Christmas is the season in the year when pulpit and press dwell, with what Emerson calls "noxious exaggeration," about the work and life, as well as the person of Jesus. We have, lying before us, the Christmas sermon of so progressive a teacher as the Rev. Jenkin Lloyd Jones. [Note: Unitarian-Independent preacher of All Souls Church, Chicago.] Here is his text: "And the Word became flesh and dwelt among us, and we beheld his glory, glory as of the only begotten from the Father."--John 1:14. How our educated neighbor can find food for sober reflection in so mystical and metaphysical an effusion, is more than we can tell. Who is the *Word* that became flesh? And when did the event take place? What does it mean to be the "only begotten from the Father?" We know what it means in the orthodox sense, but what does it mean from the Unitarian standpoint of Mr. Jones? But the text faithfully reflects the discourse which follows. It is replete with unlimited compliments to this *Word* which became flesh and assumed the name of Jesus. The following is a fair sample:

"I am compelled to think of Jesus of Nazareth as an epoch-making soul, an era-forming spirit, a character in whom the light of an illustrious race and a holy ancestry was focalized, a personality from which radiated that subtle, creative power of the spirit which defies all analysis, which baffles definition, which overflows all words."

Goodness! this is strong rhetoric, and we regret that the evidence justifying so sweeping an appreciation has been withheld from us. Although the doctor says that

Jesus "defies all analysis, baffles definition and overflows all words," he nevertheless proceeds to devote fifteen pages to the impossible task. "I am compelled to think of him as one who won the right of preeminence in the world's history," continues Mr. Jones, as if he had not said enough.

That is a definite claim, and personally, we would be glad to see it made good. But truth compels us to state that the claim is unjust. Without entering into the question of the authenticity of the gospels, a question which we have discussed at some length in our pamphlet on the "Worship of Jesus," we beg to submit that there is nothing in the gospels,--the only records which speak of him,--to entitle him to the "right of preeminence in the world's history." No one knows better than Mr. Jones that the sayings attributed to Jesus--the finest of them--are to be found in the writings of Jewish and Pagan teachers antedating the birth of Jesus by many centuries.

Was it, then, for his "works," if not for his "words," that Jesus "won the right of preeminence in the world's history"? What did he do that was not done by his predecessors? Was he the only one who worked miracles? Had the dead never been raised before? Had the blind, and the lame, and the deaf, remained altogether neglected before Jesus took compassion upon them? Moreover, what credit is there in opening the eyes of the blind or in raising the dead by miracle? Did it cost Jesus any effort to perform miracles? Did it imply a sacrifice on his part to utilize a small measure of his *infinite* power for the good of man? Who, if he could by miracle feed the hungry, clothe the naked and give light and sound to the blind and deaf, would be selfish enough not to do so? If Mr. Jones does not believe in miracles, then Jesus contributed even less than many a doctor contributes today to the welfare of the world. More poor and diseased people are visited and medicined gratuitously by a modern physician in one month, than Jesus cured miraculously in the two or three years of his career. Jesus, if he was "the only begotten of God," as Mr. Jones' text states, was not in any danger of contracting disease himself, which is not the case with the doctors and nurses who extend their services to people afflicted with contagious and abhorrent diseases. Moreover, Jesus' power must have come to him divinely, while we have to study, labor, and conquer with the sweat of our brow any power for good that we may possess. If Jesus as a God opened the eyes of the blind, would it not have been kinder if he had prevented blindness altogether? If

Jesus can open the eyes of the blind, then, why is there blindness in the world? How many of the world's multitude of sufferers did Jesus help? Which of us, if he had the divine power, would not have extended it unto every suffering child of man? Of what benefit is it to open the eyes of a few blind people, two thousand years ago, in one country, when he could, by his unique divinity, have done so much more? Mr. Jones falls into the orthodox habit of not applying to Jesus the same canons of criticism by which *human* beings are judged.

But perhaps the "preeminence of Jesus" lay in his willingness to give his life for us. Noble is every soul who prefers truth and duty to life. But was Jesus the only one, or even the first to offer himself as a sacrifice upon the altar of humanity? If Jesus died for us, how many thousands have died for him--and by infinitely more cruel deaths? It is easier for an "only begotten" of God, himself a God--who knows death can have no power over him--who sees a throne prepared for him in heaven--who is sure of rising from the dead on the third day--to face death, than for an ordinary mortal. Yet Jesus showed less courage, if his reporters are reliable, than almost any martyr whose name shines upon memory's golden page.

The European churches are full of pictures showing Jesus suffering indescribable agonies as the critical hour draws nigh. We saw, in Paris, a painting called "The Holy Face," *La Sainte Face*, which was, truly, too horrible to look upon; big tears of blood trickling down his cheeks, his head almost drooping over his chest, an expression of excruciating pain upon his features, his eyes fairly imploring for help,--he is really breaking down under the weight of his cross. Compare this picture with the serenity of Socrates drinking the hemlock in prison!

Nor would it do to say that this is only the Catholic way of representing Jesus in his passion. The picture is in the gospels, it may be seen in the Garden of Gethsemane and on the cross with all its realism. Far be it from us to withhold from Jesus, if he really suffered as the gospels report, one iota of the love and sympathy he deserves, but why convert the whole world into a black canvas upon which to throw the sole figure of Jesus? Which of us, poor, weak, sinful though we are, would not be glad to give his life, if thereby he could save a world? Do you think we would mourn and groan and weep tears of blood, or collapse, just when we should be the bravest, if we thought that by our death we would become the divine Savior of all mankind? Would we stammer, "Let this cup pass from me, if it be possible," or tear our hearts with a cry of despair: "My God, my God, why hast thou forsaken me," if we knew that the eternal welfare of the human race depended upon our death? If the Russian or Japanese soldier can take his home and wife and children,--his hopes and loves, his life,--his all,--and throw them into the mouth of the cannon, dying with a shout upon his lips,--who would hesitate to do the same, when not the salvation of one country alone, but of the whole world, depended upon it? There are examples of heroism in the annals of man which would bring the blush to the cheeks of Jesus, if his biographers have not abused his memory.

Wherein, then, was the "preeminence" of Jesus? Upon what grounds does Mr. Jones claim, with "unlimited rhetoric," to use his own expression, for Jesus "the right of preeminence in the world's history?"

While there is neither a commendable saying nor an act attributed to Jesus in our gospels which teachers older than himself had not already said or done, there are some things in which his seniors clearly outshine him. King Asoka, for instance, the Buddhist sovereign of India, 250 years before Jesus, in one of his edicts chiseled on the rocks of India, declared against human slavery and offered the sweet gift of liberty to all in captivity. Jesus used the word slave in one of his parables (improperly translated servant), without expressing himself on the subject, except to intimate that when a slave does all his duty faithfully, even then he is only an "unprofitable slave," unworthy of the thanks of his master. There was slavery of the worst kind in the world of Jesus, and yet he never opened his mouth to denounce the awful curse. It is claimed that Jesus' doctrine of love was indirectly a condemnation of slavery. Even then, inasmuch as other and earlier teachers did more than strike only indirectly at the ancient evil,--for they not only taught the brotherhood of man, too, but expressed themselves, besides, positively on the subject of slavery,--they have a prior claim to the "right of preeminence" in the world's history, if they cared anything about ranks and titles.

The doctrine of humanity to animals, our dumb neighbors, is a positive tenet in Buddhism; is it in Christianity?

Two and a half centuries before Jesus, under the influence of Buddha's teaching, King Asoka convened a religious Parliament, offering to each and every representative of other religions, absolute religious liberty. Is there any trace of such tolerance in any of the sayings of Jesus? On the contrary, the claim of Jesus that he is the light, the way, the truth, and that no man can come to the father except through him, leaves no room for the greatest of all boons--liberty, without which every promise of religion is only a mockery and a cheat. Not even heaven and eternal life can be accepted as a consideration for the loss of liberty. The liberty of teaching is alien to a teacher who claims, as Jesus did, that he alone is infallible, and that all who came before him were "thieves and robbers."

Of course, Mr. Jones will deny that Jesus ever said any of the things ascribed to him which spoil his ideal picture of him. But he finds his ideal Jesus, whose personality "defies analysis, baffles definition and overflows all words," in the gospels; if these are not reliable, what becomes of his argument? If the writers of our gospels bear false witness against Jesus when they represent him as "cursing the fig tree," as calling his enemies liars and devils, as calling the Gentiles dogs, as claiming equality with God, as menacing with damnation all who disagree with him,--what security have we that they speak truthfully when they put the beatitudes in his mouth? We have no more reliable authority for attributing to Jesus the beatitudes than we have for holding him responsible for the curses attributed to him in the gospels.

To return to our comparison between Jesus and his illustrious colleagues. It is with cheerful praise and generous pleasure that we express our admiration for many of the sayings, parables, and precepts attributed to Jesus. The fact that they are much older than Jesus, more universal than Christianity, only enhances their value and reflects glory upon the human race, a glory of which Jesus, too, as a brother, if he ever existed, has his share. We love and admire every teacher who has a message for humanity; we feel our indebtedness to them and would deem ourselves fortunate if we could contribute to the advancement of their noble influence; but we have no idols, and in our pantheon, truth is above all. We have no hesitation to sacrifice even Jesus to the Truth. If we were in India, and some Hindoo preacher spoke of Buddha, as Mr. Jones does of Jesus, as a "personality defying all analysis, baffling definition and overflowing all words"--one who has "won the right to pre-eminence in the world's history,"--we would protest against it, in the interest of Jesus and other teachers, as we now protest against Mr. Jones' Jesus, in the interest of truth. We have a suspicion, however, that if Mr. Jones, or preachers of his style, were Hindoos, they would speak of Buddha, as they now, being Christians, speak of Jesus--echoing in both instances the ***popular*** opinion.

The best way to illustrate Mr. Jones' style of reasoning is to quote a few examples from his sermon:

"The story of the Good Samaritan has had a power beyond the story of the senseless blighting of the fig tree; the ages have loved to think of Jesus talking with the woman at the well more than they have loved to think of him as manufacturing wine at Cana. No man is so orthodox but that he reads more often the Sermon on the Mount than he does the story of the drowning of the pigs."

But if he did not "drown the pigs," the reporter who says he did might have also collected from ancient sources the texts in the Sermon on the Mount and put them in Jesus' mouth.

Again:

"The dauntless crusaders who now in physical armament and again in the more invulnerable armament of the spirit, went forth, reckless of danger, regardless of cost, to rescue the world from heathen hands or to gather souls into the fold of Christ."

We can hardly believe Mr. Jones speaking of "rescuing the world from **heathen** hands," etc. Who were the heathen? And think of countenancing the craze of the crusades, which cost a million lives to possess the empty sepulchre of a mythical Savior! Is it one of the merits of Christianity that it calls other people "heathen," or that it kills them and lays waste their lands for an empty grave?

Once more:

"Jesus had tremendous expectations....He believed mightily in the future, not as some glory-rimmed heaven after death, but as a conquering kingdom of love and justice. Jesus took large stock in tomorrow; he laughed at the prudence that never dares, the mock righteousness of the ledger that presumes to balance the books and pay all accounts up to date. He knew that the prudence of commerce, the thrift of trade, the exclusive pride of the synagogue, must be broken through with a larger hope and a diviner enterprise. He believed there was to be a day after today and recognized his obligation to it; he acknowledged the debt which can never be paid to the past and which is paid only by enlarging the resources of the future. Life, to Jesus, was an open account; he was a forward looker; he was honest enough to recognize his obligations to the unborn. Perhaps this adventurous spirit in the realms of morals, even more than his heart of love, has made him the superlative leader of men."

We sincerely wish all this were true, and would be glad to have Mr. Jones furnish us with the texts or evidences which have led him to his conclusions. Would not his adjectives be equally appropriate in describing any other teacher he admires? "Jesus had tremendous expectations." Well, though this is somewhat vague as a tribute to Jesus, we presume the preacher means that Jesus was an optimist. The reports, unfortunately, flatly contradict Mr. Jones. Jesus was a "man of sorrows." He expressly declared that this earth belonged to the devil, that the road which led to destruction was crowded, while few would enter the narrow gates of life. He said: "Many are called but few are chosen;" he told his disciples to confine their good work to the lost sheep of the House of Israel, and intimated that it were not wise to take the bread of children (his people) and give it to the dogs (other people). The "Go ye into all the world" is a post- resurrection interpolation, and Mr. Jones does not believe in the miracle of the resurrection. Jesus looked forward to the speedy ending and destruction of the world, "when the sun and moon would turn black, and the stars would fall;" and he doubted whether he would find any faith in the world when "the son of man cometh"; and it was Jesus who expected to say to the people on his left, "depart from me, ye cursed, into *everlasting* punishment." This is the teacher, whose pessimism is generally admitted, of whom Mr. Jones says that, he had "tremendous expectations."

"He believed there was to be a day after today, and recognized his obligation to it," writes Mr. Jones in his indiscriminate laudation of Jesus. Is that why he said "Take no thought of the morrow," and predicted the speedy destruction of the world? "He acknowledged the debt which can never be paid to the past." A sentence like this has all the ear-marks of a glittering generality. Did Jesus show gratitude to the past when he denounced all who had preceded him in the field of love and labor as "thieves and robbers?" Equally uncertain is the following: "He was honest enough to recognize his obligations to the unborn." How does our clerical neighbor arrive at such a conclusion? From what teaching or saying of Jesus does he infer his respect for the rights of posterity? Indeed, how could a teacher who said, "He that believeth not shall be damned," he described as recognizing the rights of future generations? To menace with damnation the future inquirer or doubter is to seek to enslave as well as to insult the generations yet to be born, instead of "recognizing his obligations" to them. The Jesus Mr. Jones is writing about is not in the gospels.

"Do you ask me if I am a 'Christian'?" writes Mr. Jones, and he answers the question thus: "I do not know. Are you? If anyone is inclined to give me that high name, with the spiritual and ethical connotation in mind, I am complimented and will try to merit it." As our excellent neighbor is still in the dark, and does not know whether or not, or in what sense he is a Christian--unless he is allowed to define the word himself,--and as he also intimates that he would like to be a *Jesus* Christian, but not a Church Christian, we humbly beg to express this opinion: The American churches of today, notwithstanding all their shortcomings, are, on every question of ethics and science, of charity and the humanities, far in advance of Jesus, and that in these churches there are men and women who in breadth of mind and nobility of spirit are as good, and even better than Jesus.

Does our neighbor grasp our meaning? Charging all the bad in a religion to the account of man, and attributing all the good to God, or to a demi-god, is, after all, only a dodge. Had not the disciples of Jesus been braver than their master, his religion would not have come down to us. And had the Christian church lived up to the letter of this Semitic teacher, Europe would never have embraced Christianity. By modernizing Jesus, by selecting his more essential teachings, and relegating his eccentricities to the background, by making his name synonymous with the best aspirations of humanity, by idealizing his character and enclosing it with a human halo, the churches have saved Jesus from oblivion. Jesus was a tribal teacher, the church universalized him; Jesus had no gospel for women, the church has after much hesitation and wavering converted him to the European attitude toward women; Jesus was silent on the question of slavery, the churches have urged him with success to champion the cause of the bondsman; Jesus denounced liberty of conscience when he threatened with hell-fire the unbeliever; but the churches have won him over to the modern secular principle of religious tolerance; Jesus believed only in the salvation of the elect, but the church to a certain extent has succeeded in reconciling him to the larger hope; Jesus was an ascetic, preferring the single life to the joys of the home, and fasting and praying to the duty and privilege of labor, but the church in America and Protestant Europe at least has made Jesus a lover and a seeker of wealth and knowledge, the two great forces of civilization. No longer does Jesus say, "hate your father and mother;" no longer does he cry in our great thoroughfares, "blessed are the poor;" no longer is his voice heard denouncing this world as belonging to the devil. The modern church, modernized by science, has in turn modernized the gospels. And yet Mr. Jones prefers to be a Christian such as Jesus was. He is repeating one of those phrases which apologists use when they give God all the praise and man all the blame.

In conclusion: Mr. Jones admits that Christianity is not unique, that Buddha conquered greater tyrannies than Christ; that "humility and self-sacrifice...have world-wide foundations;" but he draws no conclusions from these important facts, but returns in a hurry to say that Jesus is the "finest and dearest stream swelling the mighty tide of history." The only objection we have to Mr. Jones' Jesus is that he is not real.

ANOTHER RHETORICAL JESUS

The Rev. W. H. H. Boyle, of St. Paul, improves even on Mr. Jones' superlative tribute to Jesus. He says:

"Can you imagine such a thing as a black sun, or the reversal of creation or the annihilation of primal light? Then, give rest to imagination and soberly think what it would mean to have the spiritual processes of two millenniums reversed, to have the light of life in the unique personally of Jesus forever eclipsed."

Here is an idolator, indeed. To make an idol of his Jesus he takes a sponge, and without a twinge of conscience, wipes out all the beauty and grandeur of the ancient world. Has this gentleman never heard of Greece? During a short existence, in only two centuries and a half, that little land of Greece achieved triumphs in the life of the mind so unparalleled as to bring all the subsequent centuries upon their knees before it. In philosophy, in poetry,--lyrical, epical, dramatic,--in sculpture, in statesmanship, in ethics, in literature, in civilization,--where is there another Greece?

Oh, land of Sophocles! whose poetry is the most perfect flower the earth has ever borne,--of Phidias and Praxiteles! whose immortal children time cannot destroy, though the gods are dead--whose masterpieces the earth wears as the best gem upon her brow,--of Aristotle! the intellect of the world,--of Socrates! the *pa-*

rens philosophiae, and its first martyr!--of Aristides! the Just--of Phocion and Epaminondas!--of Chillon and Anarcharchis! whose devotion to duty and beauty have perfumed the centuries! O, Athens, the bloom of the world! Hear this sectarian clergyman, in his black Sunday robes, closing his eyes upon all thine immortal contributions, pulling down like a vandal, as did the early Christians, the libraries and temples, the culture and civilization of the ancient world--the monuments of thy unfading glory--to build therewith a pedestal for his mythical Christ!

I can imagine the reverend advocate saying: "But there was slavery in Greece, and immorality, too,"--of course, and is the Christian world free from them? Has Christ after two thousand years abolished war? Indeed, he came to bring, as he says, "not peace, but a sword!" Has Jesus healed the world of the maladies for which we blame the Pagan world? Has he made humanity free? Has he saved the world from the fear of hell? Has he redeemed man from the blight of ignorance? Has he broken the yoke of superstition and priest-craft? Has he even succeeded in uniting into one loving fold his own disciples? How, then, can this clergyman, with any conscience for truth, compare a world deprived of the god of his sect, to a tomb--to a blind man groping under a blackened sun? Must a man rob the long past in order to provide clothing for his idol? Must he close his eyes upon all history before he can behold the beauty of his own cult?

But let us quote again:

"To efface from the statute books of Christendom every law which has its basal principle in Christian ethics; to abolish every institution which ministers to human need and misfortune in the name of Him whose sympathy is the heart of the divine; to lower every sense of moral obligation between man and man to the old level of Paganism to silence the great oratorios which have made music the echo of the divine; to take down from the galleries of the world the sacred canvases with which genius has sanctified them; to obliterate from memorial symbolism the cross of sublime renunciation which has been the rebuke of human selfishness; to disband every organization which makes prayer, through the merit of one great name, the hand of man upon the arm of God--you may be able to think of an ocean without a harbor, of a sky without a sun, of a garden without a flower, of a face without a smile, of a home without a mother; but, can you think of a world with holiness and happiness in it and Jesus gone out of it? You cannot, 'Then, come, let us adore him,'" etc., etc.

Observe how this special pleader avoids breathing so much as a word about any of the many evils which may be laid at the door of his religion with as much show of reason as the benefits he enumerates.

What about the dark ages which held all Europe for the space of a thousand years in the clutches of an ignorance the like of which no other religion in the world had known?

What about the atrocious inquisition to which no other religion in the world had ever been able to give the swing that Christianity did?

What about the persecution and burning of helpless women as witches? Is there anything as infamous as that in any religion outside of ours?

What about the wholesale massacres in the name of the true faith?

What about the centuries of religious wars, the most imbecile as well as the most bloody, from the effects of which Germany, France, Italy and England are still suffering today?

And need we also call attention to that obstinate resistance to science and progress, which rewarded every discoverer of a new power for man, with the halter or the stake, which filled the dungeons with the *elite* of Europe,--which even dug open graves to punish the bones of the dead savants and illuminators of man?

The Pagans, in their gladitorial games, sacrificed the lives of slaves: Christianity made a holocaust of the noblest intellects of Europe.

And shall we speak of the bigotry, the fanaticism, the bitter sectarian prejudices which to this day embitter the life of the world? Are not these, too, the fruits of Christianity?

We know the answer which the reverend gentleman would make to this: "All the evils you speak of are chargeable, not to Christianity, but to its abuse." But we have already shown that that argument won't do. We might as well say that all the evil of Paganism was due to its abuse. The mere fact that Christianity lent itself to such fearful distortions, and was capable of arousing the worst passions in man on such a fearful scale, is condemnation enough. It shows that there was in it a potentiality for evil beyond compare. Moreover, wherein does a "divine" religion differ from a man-made cult, if it is equally powerless to protect itself against perversion? In what sense is Jesus a god, while all his rivals were "mere men," if he is as helpless to prevent the abuse of his teachings as they were? But it would not be difficult to show that the characteristic crimes we have scheduled are the direct inspiration of a religion claiming exclusiveness and infallibility. Such texts as, "there is no other named given under heaven by which men can be saved;" "Let such an one (the man who will not be converted) be like a heathen and a publican to you;" John's advice to refrain from saying "God speed" to the alien in faith; the bible command not to "suffer a witch to live;" and many of the dogmas which might be cited,--corrupted the sympathies, perverted the judgment of the noblest, while at the same time they stung the evil- minded into something like madness. The world knew nothing of the tyranny of dogma, or religious oppression and persecution, comparatively speaking, until the advent of the Jewish-Christian Church.

"Verily I say unto you, it shall be more tolerable for the land of Sodom and of Gomorrah, in the day of judgment, than for that city," said Jesus, speaking of the people who might not accept his teachings. How can Christianity be a religion of love, and how can it believe in tolerance, when it threatens the unbeliever with a fate worse than that of Sodom and Gomorrah?

The benefits which the Rev. Boyle parades as the direct fruit of his cult, did not appear until after the Renaissance, that is to say,--the return to Pagan culture and ideals. The art and science and the humanities which he praises, followed upon the gradual decline of the Jewish-Christian religion which had already destroyed two civilizations.

But Greece and Rome triumphed. To this day, if we need models in poetry, in art, in philosophy, in literature, in politics, in patriotism, in service to the public, in heroism and devotion to ideals--we must go to the Greeks and the Romans. Not that these nations were by any means perfect, but because they have not been surpassed. In our colleges and schools, when we wish to bring up our children in the ways of wisdom and beauty, we do not give them the Christian fathers to read, we give them the Pagan classics.

We ask this St. Paul clergyman to read Gibbons' tribute to Pagan Rome: "If a man was called upon to fix a period in the history of the world during which the condition of the human race was most happy and prosperous, he would without hesitation name that which elapsed from the death of Domitian to the accession of Commodus." This period included such men and rulers as Nerva, Trajan, Adrian,

Antoninus Pius, and above all, the greatest of them all--the greatest ruler our earth has ever owned--Marcus Aurelius Antoninus. Let the Rev. W. H. H. Boyle look over the names of the kings of Israel and of Christian France, Spain, Italy and England, and find among them any one that can come up to the stature of these Pagan monarchs.

"WE OWE EVERYTHING TO JESUS"

But, behold! another clergyman with the claim that the modern world owes all its joy and cheer, during the Christmas season, "to the babe in Bethlehem." "What was it that brought about such a condition that crowds the stores, that overflows the mails, and loads the express with packages of every description? The little babe in Bethlehem set all this in motion,--the wreath, the holly, are all from him."

When we read the above and more to the same effect, we wrote to the Rev. W. A. Bartlett, [Note: Pastor First Congregational Church, Chicago.] the author of the words quoted, asking him if he was correctly reported. We reproduce herewith a copy of our letter:

DEC, 20, 1904. ***Rev. W. A. Bartlett, Washington Boul. and Ann St., Chicago***

DEAR MR. BARTLETT: In the report of your sermon of last Sunday you are represented as claiming that it is to the "babe in Bethlehem" we owe the Christmas festival, the giving of presents, etc., etc. I write to ascertain whether this report has stated your position correctly? I am sure you know that Christmas is only a recomposition of an old Pagan festival, and that "giving presents" at this season is a much older practice than Christianity. Of course, you do not believe that Christmas is celebrated in December and on the 25th of the month because Jesus was born on that day. You know as well as I do of the Pagan festivals celebrated in the month of December throughout the Roman Empire--celebrations which were accompanied with the giving and receiving of presents. Moreover, you know also, as every student does, that in the Latin countries of Europe it is not on Christmas day, but on New Year's day, that presents are exchanged. Surely you would not claim that for New Year's day, too, the world is indebted to the Bethlehem babe. You must also have known that the use of the evergreen and the holy was in vogue among the Druids of Pagan times. Be kind enough, therefore, to give me, if I am not asking too much, the facts which led you to make the statement to which I have called your attention, and believe me, with great respect, etc.

To this neighborly letter the reverend gentleman did not condescend to send an acknowledgment. We knocked at his door, as it were, and he, a minister of the Gospel, declined to open it unto us. Clergymen, as a rule, say that they are happy when people will let them preach the gospel to them. In our case, we saved the clergyman from calling upon us, we called upon him--that is to say, we wrote and gave him an opportunity to enlighten us, to bring his influence to bear upon us, to open our eyes to the error of our ways,--and he would have nothing to do with us. Was not our soul worth saving? Did the Rev. W. A. Bartlett consider us beyond hope? We ask this clergyman to place his hand upon his conscience and ask himself whether he did the brotherly thing in not returning a friendly and kindly answer to our honest inquiry for truth. But he did not answer us, because he had no real faith in his gospel. It was not good enough for an inquirer.

But the clergyman, according to reports, made an attempt on the Sunday following the receipt of our letter, before his congregation, to answer indirectly our question. He denied that "Christmas was a recomposition of an old Pagan festival," and said that the early Christians "fasted and wept" because of these Pagan festivals, and that as early as the second century, the birth of Jesus was commemorated. In short, he pronounced it "a distortion of history" to assign to the Christmas festival a Pagan origin. In his great work on the *History of Civilization,* Buckle says this, to which we call Dr. Bartlett's attention: "As soon as eminent men grown unwilling to enter any profession, the luster of that profession will be tarnished; first its reputation will be lessened, then its power abridged." We fear this is true of Mr. Bartlett's profession.

How can Christian ministers hope to engage the interest of the reading public if they themselves abstain from reading? Ask a secular newspaper about the origin of the Christmas celebration, and *it* will tell you the truth. On the very Sunday that Dr. Bartlett was denouncing, in his church, our claim that the Pagans gave us the December season of joy and merry-making, as "a distortion of history," and editorial in the *Chicago Tribune* said this:

But the festive character of the celebration, the giving of presents, the feasting and merriment, the use of evergreen and holly and mistletoe, are all remnants of Pagan rites.

Continuing, the same editorial called attention to the antiquity of the institution:

Long before the shepherds on the Judean plains saw the star rise in the east and heard the tidings of "Peace on earth, good will to man," the Roman populace surged through the streets at the feast of Saturn, giving themselves up to wild license and boisterous merry making. They exchanged presents, they decorated their dwellings and temples with green boughs; slaves were given special privileges, and the spirit of good will was abroad among men. This Roman Saturnalia came at the winter solstice, the same as does our Christmas day, while the birth of Christ is widely believed to have taken place at some other season of the year.

But Dr. Bartlett may have had in mind the quotation from Anastasius:

"Our Lord, Jesus Christ, was born of the Holy Virgin, Mary, in Bethlehem, at one o'clock in the afternoon of December 25th,"--appearing to quote from some old manuscript which, unfortunately, is not to be found anywhere. But Clement of Alexandria, in the year 210 A. D., dismisses all guesses as to when Jesus was born,--the 18th of April, 19th of May, etc.,--as products of reckless speculation. March 28th is given as Jesus' birthday in *De Pascha Computius*, in the year 243. Jan. 5th is the date defended by Epiphanius. Baradaens, Bishop of Odessa, says: "No one knows exactly the day of the nativity of our Lord: this only is certain from what Luke writes, that he was born in the night." Poor Dr. Bartlett, his December 25th does not receive support from the Fathers.

For our clerical brother's sake, we quote some more from the *Tribune* editorial:

Primeval man looked upon the sun as the revelation of divinity. When the shortest day of the year was passed, when the sun began his march northward, the primitive man rejoiced in the thought of the coming seedtime and summer, and he made feasts and revelry the mode of expressing the gladness of his heart. Among the sun worshipers of Persia, among the Druids of the far north, among the Phoenicians, among the Romans, and among the ancient Goths and Saxons the winter solstice was the occasion of festivities. Many of them were rude and barbarous, but they were all distinguished by hearty and profuse hospitality.

And yet our neighbor calls it "distortion of history" to connect Christmas with the Pagan festival, celebrated about this time. We quote once more from the Secular press:

The Christian church did not abolish these heathen ceremonies, but grafted upon them a deeper spiritual meaning. For this reason Christmas is an institution which memorializes the best there was in Pagan man. Its good cheer, its charity, its sports, its feasting, and the features which most endear it to children are all the heritage of our Pagan ancestors.

How refreshing this, compared with the clergyman's silence, or cry of "distortion." But in one thing the doctor is correct. The early Christians did bewail the Pagan festivals, as they did everything else that was Pagan. But it did not help them at all; they were compelled to acquiesce. The Christians have "fasted and prayed" also against science, progress, and modern thought, but what good has it done? They asked God to hook Theodore Parker's tongue; to overthrow Darwin, and to confound the wisdom of this world, but the prayer remains unanswered. Yes, the doctor is right, the church has "fasted and prayed" against religious tolerance, against the use of Sunday as a day of recreation,--the opening of galleries and libraries on that day, the advancement of women, the emancipation of the negro, the secularization of education, the revision of old creeds, and a thousand other things. But their opposition has only damaged their own cause. They did try to suppress the Pagan festival, which we call Christmas, and the Puritans in this country, until recently, abstained from all recognition of the day, and called it "Popery," and "Paganism," but their efforts bore no fruit. Dr. Bartlett, if he will read, will learn that for many years, in England and in this country, the observance of Christmas was forbidden by law under severe penalties. As to our being indebted for the cheer and merriment of the December festival to the "Bethlehem babe," the doctor must inform himself of those acts of Parliament which, under the Puritan regime, compelled people to mourn on Christmas day and to abstain from merrymaking. In Christian Connecticut, for a man to have a sprig of holly in his house on Christmas day was a finable crime. In Massachusetts, any Christian detected celebrating Christmas was fined five shillings and costs. But, see, having failed to suppress these good institutions, they now turn about and claim that they have always believed in them, and that, in fact, we would not now be enjoying any one of these benefits but for the Christian Church.

In conclusion, we have one other word to say to the three clerical teachers from whose writings we have quoted. Against them we are constrained to bring the charge of looseness in thought. They seem to have little conscience for evidence. Mr. Jones says, for instance:

"In short, I am compelled to think that this Light of Souls, this saving and redeeming spirit, was the loved and loving child of Joseph, the carpenter, and the loyal wife Mary. I believe this, notwithstanding the stories of immaculate conceptions, star-guided magi, choiring angels and adoring shepards that gathered around the birth-night."

Which is another way of saying that he is "compelled to believe" against the evidence, merely because it is his pleasure or interest to do so. This is not very edifying, to be sure. Mr. Jones takes all his information about Joseph and Mary and Jesus from the gospels, and yet the gospels clearly contradict his conclusions. Mary, the mother of Jesus, gives her word of honor that Joseph was not the father of her child, and Joseph himself testifies that he is not Jesus' father, but Mr. Jones pays no attention to their testimony; he wishes Joseph to be the father of Jesus, and that ought to be sufficient evidence, he thinks. We quote from the gospel:

"Now the birth of Jesus Christ was on this wise: When his mother Mary had been betrothed to Joseph, before they came together she was found with child of the Holy Ghost. And Joseph, her husband, being a righteous man, and not willing to make her a public example, was minded to put her away privily. But when he thought on these things, behold, an angel of the Lord appeared unto him in a dream, saying, Joseph, thou son of David, fear not to take unto thee Mary thy wife; for that which is conceived in her is of the Holy Ghost."

Now, if Joseph admits he was not Jesus' father, and Mary corroborates his testimony (See Luke, 1st chapter), Jesus was, if he ever lived, and the records which give Mr. Jones his ideal Jesus are reliable, the son of a man who has succeeded in concealing his identity, unless, of course, we believe in the virgin birth. If the real father of Jesus had come forth and owned his son, and Mary had acknowledged that he was the father of her child, what would have become of Christianity? We hope these clergymen who have dwelt, as Emerson says, "with noxious exaggeration about the person of Jesus," will reflect upon this, and while doing so, will they not also remember this other saying of the Concord philosopher: "The vice of our theology is seen in the claim...that Jesus was something different from a man."

We take our leave of the three clergymen, assuring them that in what we have said we have not been actuated, in the least, by any personal motive whatever, and that we have only done to them what we would have them do to us.

A LIBERAL JEW ON JESUS FELIX ADLER, PRAISES JESUS

That it is very easy for scholars to follow the people instead of leading them, and to side with the view that commands the majority, receives fresh confirmation from the recent utterances of the founder of the Ethical Culture Society in New York. Professor Adler, the son of a rabbi, and at one time a freethinker, has slowly drifted into orthodox waters, after having tried for a period of years the open seas, and has become a more enthusiastic champion of the god of the Christians than many a Christian scholar whom we could name. The pendulum in the Adler case has swung clear to the opposite side. We do not find fault with a man because he changes his views, we only ask for reasons for the change. It will be seen by the following extracts from Adler's printed lectures that he has made absolutely no critical study of the sources of the Jesus story, but has merely, and hurriedly at that, accepted the conventional estimate of Jesus and enlarged upon it. Jesus is entitled to all the praise which is due him, but it must first be shown that in praising him we are not sacrificing the truth. Praising any man at such a cost is merely flattering the masses and bowing to the fashion of the day.

Let us hear what Professor Adler has to say about Jesus. He writes:

It has been said that if Christ came to New York or Chicago, they would stone him in the very churches. It is not so! If Christ came to New York or Chicago, the publicans and sinners would sit at his feet! For they would know that he cared for them better than they in their darkness knew how to care for themselves, and they would love him as they loved him in the days of yore.

This would sound pious in the mouth of a Moody or a Torrey, but, we confess, it sounds like affectation in the mouth of the free thinking son of a rabbi. That Prof. Adler enters here into a field for which his early Jewish training has not fitted him, is apparent from the hasty way in which he has put his sentences together. "It has been said," he writes, "that if Christ came to New York or Chicago, they would stone him in the very churches. It is not so." Why is it not so? And he answers: "If Christ came to New York or Chicago, the publicans and sinners would sit at his feet." But what has the reception which publicans and sinners might give Jesus to do with how *the churches* would receive him? He proves that Jesus would not be stoned in the churches of New York and Chicago by saying that the "publicans and sinners would sit at his feet." Does he mean that "New York and Chicago churches" and "publicans and sinners" are the same thing? "Publicans and sinners" might welcome him, and still the churches might stone him, which in fact, according to Adler's own admission, was the case in Jerusalem, where the synagogues conspired against Jesus, while Mary Magdalene sat at his feet. Nor are his words about "the publicans and sinners loving Jesus as they loved him in the days of yore" edifying. Who does he mean by the "publicans and sinners," and how many of them loved Jesus in the days of yore, and why should this class of people have felt a special love for him?

On the question of the resurrection of Jesus, Prof. Adler says this:

"It is sometimes insinuated that the entire Christian doctrine depends on the accounts contained in the New Testament, purporting that Jesus actually rose on the third day and was seen by his followers; and that if these reports are found to be contradictory, unsupported by sufficient evidence, and in themselves incredible, then the bottom falls out of the belief in immortality as represented by Christianity."

It was the Apostle Paul himself who said that "if Jesus has not risen from the dead, then is our faith in vain,--and we are, of all men, most miserable." So, you see, friend Adler, it is not "sometimes insinuated," as you say, but it is openly, and to our thinking, logically asserted, that if Jesus did not rise from the dead, the whole fabric of Christian eschatology falls to the ground. But we must remember that Prof. Adler has not been brought up a Christian. He has acquired his Christian predilections only recently, so to speak, hence his unfamiliarity with its Scriptures. Continuing, the Professor says:

"But similar reports have arisen in the world time and again, apparitions of the dead have been seen and have been taken for real; and yet such stories, after being current for a time, invariably have passed into oblivion. Why did this particular story persist, despite the paucity and the insufficiency of the evidence? Why did it get itself believed and take root?"

What shall we think of such reasoning from the platform of a presumable rationalist movement? Does not the Professor know that the story of the resurrection of Jesus is not original, but a repetition of older stories of the kind? Had the world never heard of such after- death apparitions before Jesus' day, it would never have invented the story of his resurrection. And how does the Professor know that the story of Jesus' resurrection is not going to meet the same fate which has overtaken all other similar stories? Is it not already passing into the shade of neglect? Are not the intelligent among the Christians themselves beginning to explain the resurrection of Jesus allegorically, denying altogether that he rose from the dead in a literal sense? Moreover, the pre-Christian stories of similar resurrections lived to an old age,--two or three thousand years--before they died, and the story of Jesus' resurrection has yet to prove its ability to live longer. All miraculous beliefs are disappearing, and the story of the Christian resurrection will not be an exception. But Prof. Adler's motive in believing that the story of the resurrection of Jesus shall live, is to offer it as an argument for immortality, and in so doing he strains the English language in lauding Jesus. He says:

"In my opinion, people believed in the resurrection of Jesus because of the precedent conviction in the minds of the disciples that such a man as Jesus could not die, because of the conviction that a personality of such superlative excellence, so radiant, so incomparably lofty in mien and port and speech and intercourse with others, could not pass away like a forgotten wind, that such a star could not be quenched."

We regret to say that there are as many assumptions in the above sentence as there are lines in it. Of course, if we are for emotionalism and not for exact and accurate conclusions, Adler's estimate of Jesus is as rhetorical as that of Jones or Boyle, but if we have any love for historical truth, there is not even the shadow of evidence, for instance, that the disciples could not believe "that such a man as Jesus could die." On the contrary, the disciples left him at the cross and fled, and believed him dead, until it was reported to them that he had been seen alive, and even then "some doubted," and one wished to feel the flesh with his fingers before he would credit his eyes. Jesus had to eat and drink with them, he had to "open their eyes," and perform various miracles before they would believe that he was not dead. The text which says that the apostles hesitated to believe in the resurrection because "as yet they knew not the scripture, that he would rise from the dead," shows conclusively how imaginary is the idea that there was a "precedent conviction" in the minds of the disciples that such a man as Jesus could not die. Apparently it was all a matter of prophecy, not of moral character at all. Yet in the face of all the evidence to the contrary, Prof. Adler tells his Carnegie Hall audience, who unfortunately are even less informed in Christian doctrine than their leader, that "there was a precedent conviction in the minds of the disciples that such a man as Jesus could not die." And what gave the disciples this supposed "precedent conviction?" "That a personality of such superlative excellence, so radiant, so incomparably lofty in mien and port and speech and intercourse with others, could not pass away like a forgotten wind, that such a star could not be quenched." We are simply astonished, and grieved as well, to see the use which so enlightened a man as Prof. Adler makes of his gifts. Will this Jewish admirer of the god of Christendom kindly tell us wherein Jesus was superlatively excellent, or incomparably lofty in mien and port and speech and intercourse with others? Was there a weakness found in men like Buddha, Confucius, Socrates, etc., from which Jesus was free? That Jesus created no such ideal impression upon his disciples, is shown by the fact that they represented him as a sectarian and an egotist who denounced all who had preceded him as unworthy of respect and to be despised. And how could a man whose public life did not cover more than two or three years of time, and who lived as a celibate and a monk, returning every night to his cave in the Mount of Olives, taking no active part in the business life-- supporting no family or parents, assuming no civil or social duties--how can such a man, we ask, be held up as a model for the men and women of today? Jesus, according to his biographers, believed he could raise the dead, and announced himself the equal of God. "I and my father are one," he is reported to have said; and one of his apostles writes: "He (Jesus) thought it no robbery to be equal to God." Either this report is true, or it is not. If it is, what shall we think of a man who thought he was a god and could raise the dead? If the report is not true, what reliance can we place in his biographers when the things which they affirm with the greatest confidence are to be rejected?

Yet Prof. Adler, swept off his feet by the popular and conventional enthusiasm about Jesus, describes him as "a personality of such superlative excellence, so radiant, so incomparably lofty in mien and port and speech and intercourse with others," that his followers could not believe he was a mere mortal. But where is the Jesus to correspond to this rhetorical language? He is not in the anonymous gospels. There we find only a fragmentary character patched or pieced together, as it were, by various contributors--a character made up of the most contradictory elements, as we have tried to show in the preceding pages. The Jesus of Adler is not in history, he is not even in mythology. There is no one of that name and answering that description in the four gospels.

That a loose way of speaking grows upon one if one is not careful, and that sounding phrases and honest historical criticism are not the same thing, will be seen by Prof. Adler's lavish praise of John Calvin. He speaks of him in terms almost as glowing as he does of Jesus. He calls Calvin "that mighty and noble man."

That Calvin ruled Geneva like a Russian autocrat; that he was "mighty" in a community in which Jacques Gruet was beheaded because he had "danced," and also because he had committed the grave offense of saying that "Moses was only a man and no one knows what God said to him," and in which Michael Servetus was burned alive for holding opinions contrary to those which the Genevan pope was interested in,--is readily conceded. But was Calvin "mighty" in a beneficent sense? Did his power save people from the Protestant inquisition? Was not the Geneva of his day called *the Protestant Rome?* And if he did not use his powerful influence to further religious tolerance and intellectual honesty; if he did not use his position to save men from the grip of superstition and the fear of hell, how can Prof. Adler refer to him as "that mighty and noble man--John Calvin?"

It is not our purpose to grudge Calvin any compliments which Felix Adler wishes to pay him. What we grieve to see is, that he should, indirectly at least, recommend to the admiration of his readers a man who, if he existed today and acted as he did in the Geneva of the sixteenth century, would be regarded by every morally and intellectually awakened man, as a criminal. Has not Felix Adler examined the evidence which incriminates Calvin and proves him beyond doubt as the murderer of Servetus? "If he (Servetus) comes to Geneva, I shall see that he does not escape alive," wrote John Calvin to Theodore Beza. And he carried out his fearful menace; Servetus was put to death by the most horrible punishment ever invented--he was burned alive in a smoking fire. What did this mighty and noble man do to save a stranger and a scholar from so atrocious a fate? Let his eulogist, Prof. Adler, answer. It will not do to say that those were different times. A thousand voices were raised against the wanton and cruel murder of Servetus, but Calvin's was not among them. In fact, when Calvin himself was a fugitive and a wanderer, he had written in favor of religious tolerance, but no sooner did he become the Protestant pope of Geneva, than he developed into an exterminator of heresy by fire. Such is the "mighty and noble man" held up for our admiration. "Mighty" he was, but we ask again, was he mighty in a noble sense?

Had Calvin been considered a "mighty and noble man" by the reformers who preceded Prof. Adler, there would have been no Ethical Culture societies in America today. Prof. Adler is indebted for the liberties which he enjoys in New York to the Voltaires and the Condorcets, who regarded Calvin and his "isms" as pernicious to the intellectual life of Europe, and did all they could to lead the people away from them. Think of the leader of the Ethical Societies exalting a persecutor, to say nothing of his abominable theology, or of his five *aliases,* as "that mighty and noble man;--John Calvin!" We feel grateful to Prof. Adler for organizing the Ethical Societies in American, but we would be pleased to have him explain in what sense a man of Calvin's small sympathies and terrible deeds could be called both "noble and mighty." [Note: See "The Kingdom of God in Geneva Under Calvin."--M. M. Mangasarian.]

It was predicted some years ago that the founder of the Ethical Societies will before long return to the Jewish faith of his fathers. However this may be, we have seen, in his estimate of Jesus and John Calvin, evidences of his estrangement from rationalism, of which in his younger days he was so able a champion. In his criticism of the Russian scientist, Metchnikoff, of the Pasteur Institute in Paris, Prof. Adler, endorsing the popular estimate of Jesus, accepts also the popular attitude toward science. He appears to prefer the doctrine of special creation to the theory of evolution. We would not have believed this of Felix Adler if we did not have the evidence before us. We speak of this to show the relation between an exaggerated praise of a popular idol, and a denial of the conclusions of modern science. It is the popular view which Prof. Adler champions in both instances. In his criticism of Metchnikoff's able book, *The Nature of Man,* Prof. Adler writes:

And to account for the reason in man, this divine spark that has been set ablaze in him, it is not sufficient to point to an ape as our ancestor. If we are descended from an anthropoid ape on the physical side, we are not descended from him in any strict sense of the word on our rational side; for as life is born of life, so reason is born of reason, and if the anthropoid ape does not possess reason as we possess it, it cannot be said that on our rational side we are his progeny.

If the above had been written fifty years ago, when the doctrine of evolution was a heresy, or by an orthodox clergyman of today, we would have taken no note of it. But coming as it does from the worthy founder of the Ethical Movement in America, it deserves attention. "If," says Dr. Adler, "we are descended from an anthropoid ape on the physical side, we are not descended from him in any strict sense of the word on our rational side." He is not sure, evidently, that even physically man is the successor of the anthropoid ape, but he is sure that "we are not descended from him...on our rational side." Is Dr. Adler, then, a dualist? Does he believe that there are two eternal sources, from one of which we get our bodies, and from the other our "rational side?" And why cannot Dr. Adler be a monist? He answers, "for as life is born of life, so reason is born of reason, and if the anthropoid ape does not possess reason as we possess it, it cannot be said that on our rational side we are his progeny." Not so, good doctor! There is no life without reason. Do we mean to say that the jelly-fish, the creeping worm, or the bud on the tree has reason? Yes; not as much reason as a horse or a dog, and certainly not as much as a Metchnikoff or an Adler, but these lower forms of life could not have survived but for the element of rationality in them. We may call this instinct, sensation, promptings of nature, but what's in a name? The difference between a pump and a watch is only a difference of mechanism. The stone and the soul represent different stages of progression, not different substances. If a charcoal can be transformed into a diamond, why may not nature, with the resources of infinity at her command, refine a stone into a soul? Let us not marvel at this; it is not less thinkable than the proposition of two independent sources of life, the one physical, the other rational. If "life is born of life," where did the first life come from? Let us have an answer to that question. And if, as the professor says, "reason is born of reason," how did the first reason come? Is it not very much simpler to think in monistic terms, than to separate life from reason, and mind from matter, as Prof. Adler does in the words quoted above? Why cannot mind be a state of matter? What objection is there to thinking that matter, refined, elevated, ripened, cultured, becomes both sentient and rational? If matter can feel, can see, can hear, can it not also think? Does not the horse see, hear and think? There is no lowering of the dignity of man to say that he tastes with his palate, sees with his eyes, hears with his ears, and thinks with the gray matter in his brain. Remove his optic nerve and he becomes blind, destroy the ganglia in his brain, and he becomes mindless. Gold is as much matter as the dust, but it is very much more precious; so is mind infinitely more precious than the matter which can only feel, see, taste or hear. "If the anthropoid ape does not possess reason as we possess it, it cannot be said that on our rational side we are his progeny," says Dr. Adler: But, suppose we were to say that if our remote African or Australian savage ancestors did not possess reason as we possess it, "it cannot be said that on our rational side we are their progeny," The child in the cradle does not possess reason "as we do," any more than does the anthropoid ape, but the beginnings of reason are in both. Let the worm climb and he will overtake man. This is a most hopeful, a most beautiful gospel. Its spirit is not one of isolation and exclusiveness from the rest of nature, but one of fellowship and sympathy. We are all--plants, trees, birds, bugs, animals--all members of one family, children at various ages and stages of growth of the same great mother,--Nature. We quote again:

"When I ask him (Metchnikoff) whence do I come, he points to the simian stage which we have left behind; but I would look beyond that stage to some ultimate fount of being, to which all that is highest in me and in the world around me can be traced, a source of things equal to the best that I can conceive."

But if there is "some ultimate fount of being," to which our "highest" nature "can be traced," whence did our lower nature come? Is Prof. Adler trying to say God? We do not object to the word, we only ask that he give the word a more intelligible meaning than has yet been given. If God is the "ultimate fount of being to which all that is highest in us can be traced," who or what is the ultimate fount to which all that is lowest in us can be traced? Let us have the names of the two ultimate founts of being, and also to what still more ultimate founts *these* founts may be traced.

In our opinion Dr. Adler has failed to do justice to Prof. Metchnikoff. It is no answer to the Darwinian Theory, which the Russian scientist accepts in earnest, and in all its fullness,--not fractionally, as Adler seems to do--to say that it does not explain everything. No one claims that it does. Not all the mystery of life has been cleared. Evolution has offered us only a new key, so to speak, with which to attempt the doors which have not yielded to metaphysics. And if the key has not opened all the doors, it has opened many. Prof. Adler seems to think that the doctrine of evolution explains only the physical descent of man; for the genesis of the spiritual man, he looks for some supernatural "fount" in the skies. Well, that is not science; that is theology, and Adler's estimate of Jesus is just as theological as his criticism of evolution.

APPENDIX

The argument in this volume will be better understood if we give to our readers the comments and criticisms which our little pamphlet, ***Jesus a Myth,*** and ***The Mangasarian-Crapsey Debate on the Historicity of Jesus,*** [Note: Price, 25c. Independent Religious Society, Orchestra Hall, Chicago.] called forth from orthodox and liberal clergymen. We shall present these together with our reply as they appeared on the Sunday Programs of the Independent Religious Society.

Criticism is welcome. If the criticism is just, it prevents us from making the same mistake twice; if it is unjust, it gives us an opportunity to correct the error our critic has fallen into. No one's knowledge is perfect. But the question is, does a teacher suppress the facts? Does he insist on remaining ignorant of the facts?

FROM THE SUNDAY PROGRAMS
I

Now that the debate on one of the most vital questions of modern religious thought--The Historicity of Jesus--is in print, a few further reflections on some minor points in Dr. Crapsey's argument may add to the value of the published copy.

REV. DR. CRAPSEY: "Now, I say this is the great law of religious variation, that in almost every instance, indeed, I think, in every single instance in history, all such movements begin with a ***single*** personality." (P. 5, ***Mangasarian-Crapsey***

Debate.)

ANSWER: The only way this question can be settled is by appealing to history. Mithraism is a variant religion, which at one time spread over the Roman Empire and came near outclassing Christianity. Yet, Mithra, represented as a young man, and worshiped as a god, is a myth. How, then, did Mithraism arise?

Religions, as well as their variations, appear as new branches do upon an old tree. The new branch is quite as much the product of the soil and climate as the parent tree. Like Brahmanism, Judaism, Shinto and the Babylonian and Egyptian Cults, which had no *single* founders, Christianity is a *deposit* to which Hellenic, Judaic and Latin tendencies have each contributed its quota.

But the popular imagination craves a Maker for the Universe, a founder for Rome, a first man for the human race, and a great chief as the starter of the tribe. In the same way it fancies a divine, or semi- divine being as the author of its *credo.*

Because Mohammed is historical, it does not follow that Moses is also historical. That argument would prove too much.

REV. DR. CRAPSEY: "We would be in the same position that the astronomers were when they discovered the great planet Uranus--from their knowledge of the movements of these bodies they were convinced that these perturbations could be occasioned by nothing less than a great planet lying outside of the then view of mankind."(P. 6, *Ibid.*)

ANSWER: But the astronomers did not rest until they converted the *probability* of a near-by planet into *demonstration.* Jesus is still a probability.

REV. DR. CRAPSEY: "We have of Jesus a very distinctly outlined history. There is nothing vague about him." (P. 12, *Ibid*.)

ANSWER: But in the same sentence the doctor takes all this back by adding: "There are a great many things in his history that are not historical." If so, then we do not possess "a very distinctly outlined history," but at best a mixture of fact and fiction.

REV. DR. CRAPSEY: "We can follow Jesus' history from the time that he entered upon his public career until the time that career closed, just as easily as we can follow Caesar, etc." (P. 12, *Ibid*.)

ANSWER: How long was "the time from the opening of Jesus' public career until the time that it closed?"--One year!--according to the three gospels. It sounds quite a period to speak of "following his public career" from beginning to end, especially when compared with Caesar's, until it is remembered that the entire public career of Jesus covers the space of only one year. This is a most decisive argument against the historicity of Jesus. With the exception of one year, his whole life is hid in impenetrable darkness. We know nothing of his childhood, nothing of his old age, if he lived to be old, and of his youth, we know just enough to fill up a year. Under the circumstances, there is no comparison between the public career of a Caesar or a Socrates covering from fifty to seventy years of time, and that of a Jesus of whose life only one brief year is thrown upon the canvas.

An historical Jesus who lived only a year!

REV. DR. CRAPSEY: The Christ I admit to be purely mythological....the word Christ, you know, means the anointed one....they (the Hebrews) expected the coming of that Christ....But that is purely a mythical title. (*The Debate*--P. 35.)

ANSWER: Did the Hebrews then expect the coming of a *title?* Were they looking forward to seeing the ancient throne of David restored by a *title?* By Messiah or Christ the Jews did not mean a *name,* but a man--a real flesh and bone savior, anointed or appointed by heaven.

But if the 'Christ' which the Hebrews expected was "purely mythical," what makes the same 'Christ' in the supposed Tacitus passage historical? The New Testament Jesus is Jesus Christ, and the apostle John speaks of those "who confess not that Jesus Christ is come in the flesh"--mark his words--not Christ, but *Jesus Christ.* The apostle does not separate the two names. There were those, then, in the early church who denied the historicity, not of a *title*,--for what meaning would there be in denying that a *title* "is come in the flesh,"--but of a person, known as *Jesus Christ.*

And what could the doctor mean when he speaks of a *title* being "mythological?" There are no mythological titles. Titles are words, and we do not speak of the historicity or the non-historicity of words. We cannot say of words as we do of men, that some are historical and others are mythical. William Tell is a myth--not the name, but the man the name stands for. *William* is the name of many real people, and so is *Tell.* There were many anointed kings, who are historical, and the question is, Is Jesus Christ--or Jesus the Anointed--also historical? To answer that

Jesus is historical, but The Anointed is not, is to evade the question.

When Mosheim declares that "The prevalent opinion among early Christians was that Christ existed in appearance only," he could not have meant by 'Christ' only a title. There is no meaning in saying that a man's title "existed in appearance only?"

We do not speak of a title being born, or crucified; and when some early Christians denied that Jesus Christ was ever born or ever crucified, they had in mind not a *title* but a *person.*

In conclusion: If the 'Christ' by whom the Hebrews meant, not a mere name, but a man, was "purely mythological," as the reverend debater plainly admits (see pages 35, 36 of *The Debate*)--that is, if when the Hebrews said: "Christ *is* coming," they were under the influence of an illusion,--why may not the Christians when they say that 'Christ' *has* come, be also under the influence of an illusion? The Hebrew illusion said, Christ was coming; the Christian illusion says, Christ has come. The Hebrews had no evidence that 'Christ' was coming, although that expectation was a great factor in their religion; and the Christians have no more evidence for saying 'Christ' has come, although that belief is a great factor in *their* religion.

II

The minister of the South Congregational Church, who heard the debate, has publicly called your lecturer an "unscrupulous sophist," who "practices imposition upon a popular audience" and who "put forth sentence after sentence which every scholar present knew to be a perversion of the facts so outrageous as to be laughable."

As one of the leading morning papers said, the above "is not a reply to arguments made by Mr. Mangasarian."

Invited by several people to prove these charges, the Reverend replies: "In the absence of any full report of what he (M. M. Mangasarian) said, or of any notes taken at the time, I am unable to furnish you with quotations." When the Reverend gentleman was addressing the public his memory was strong enough to enable him to say, "sentence after sentence was put forth by Mr. Mangasarian which every scholar present knew to be a perversion of the facts." But when called upon to mention a few of them, his memory forsakes him. Our critic is not careful to make his statements agree with the fact.

One instance, however, he is able to remember which "when it fell upon my ears," he writes, "it struck me with such amazement, that it completely drove from my mind a series of most astonishing statements of various sorts which had just preceded it."

We refrain from commenting on the excuse given to explain so significant a failure of memory. The instance referred to was about the denial of some in apostolic times that "Jesus Christ is come in the flesh." But as Mr. Mangasarian had hardly spoken more than twenty minutes when he touched upon this point, it is not likely that it could have been "preceded by a series of most astonishing statements of various sorts."

And what was the statement which, while it crippled his memory, it did not moderate his zeal? We will let him present it himself; "I refer to the use he made of one or two passages in the New Testament, mentioning some who deny 'that Jesus Christ is come in the flesh.' 'So that,' he went on to say, 'there were those even among the early Christians themselves who denied that Jesus had come in the flesh. Of course, they were cast out as heretics.' *Here came an impressive pause,* and then without further explanation or qualification, he proceeded to something else."

This is his most serious complaint. Does it justify hasty language?

St. John writes of those who "confessed not that Jesus Christ is come in the flesh." The natural meaning of the words is that even in apostolic times some denied the flesh and bone Jesus, and regarded him as an idea or an apparition--something like the Holy Ghost. All church historians admit the existence of sects that denied the New Testament Jesus--the Gnostics, the Essenes, the Ebionites, the Marcionites, the Cerinthians, etc.

As the debate is now in print, further comment on this would not be necessary.

Incidents like the above, however, should change every lukewarm rationalist into a devoted soldier of truth and honor.

To us, more important than anything presented on this subject, is this evidence of the existence of a very early dispute among the first disciples of Jesus on the question of whether he was real or merely an apparition. The Apostle John, in his epistle, clearly states that even among the faithful there were those *who confess not that Jesus Christ is come in the flesh.* This is very important. As early as John's time, if he is the writer of the epistle, Jesus' historicity was questioned.

The gospel of John also hints at the existence in the primitive church of Christians who did not accept the reality of Jesus. When doubting Thomas is told of the resurrection, he answers that he must feel the prints of the nails with his fingers before he will believe, and Jesus not only grants the wishes of this skeptical apostle, but he also eats in the presence of them all, which story is told evidently to silence the critics who maintained that Jesus was only a spirit, "the Wisdom of God," an emanation, a light, and not real flesh and bones.

III

The same clergyman, to whom a copy of the *Mangasarian-Crapsey Debate* was sent, has written a five page criticism of it.

The strength of a given criticism is determined by asking: Does it in any way impair the soundness of the argument against which it is directed? Critics have discovered mistakes in Darwin and Haeckel, but are these mistakes of such a nature as to prove fatal to the theory of evolution?

To be effective, criticism must be aimed at the *heart* of an argument. A man's life is not in his hat, which could be knocked off, or in his clothes--which could be torn in places by his assailant without in the least weakening his opponent's position. It is the blow that disables which counts.

To charge that we have said 'Gospel,' where we should have said 'Epistle,' or 'Trullum' instead of 'Trullo'; that it was not Barnabas, but Nicholas who denied the Gospel Jesus, and that there were variations of this denial, does not at all disprove the fact that, according to the Christian scriptures themselves, among the apostolic followers there were those to whom Jesus Christ was only a phantom.

Milman, the Christian historian, states that the belief about Jesus Christ "adopted by almost all the Gnostic sects," was that Jesus Christ *was but an apparent human being, an impassive phantom,* (*History of Christianity.* Vol. 2, P. 61). Was ever such a view entertained of Caesar, Socrates or of any other historical character?

On page 28 of *The Debate* we say: "The Apostle John complains of those....who confess not that Jesus Christ is come in the flesh." To this the clergyman replies:

"The Apostle John never made any such complaint. Critical scholarship is pretty well agreed that he did not write the epistles ascribed to him."

We have a lecture on "How the Bible was Invented," and this clergyman's admission that at least parts of the bible *are* invented is very gratifying.

In a former communication, this same clergyman tried to prove that the Apostle John's complaint does not at all imply a denial of the historical Jesus. In his recent letter he denies that the apostle ever made such a complaint.

John did not write the epistles, then, which the Christian church for two thousand years, and at a cost of millions of dollars, and at the greater sacrifice of truth and progress has been proclaiming to the world as the work of the inspired John!

The strenuous efforts to get around this terrible text in the "Holy Bible," show what a decisive argument it is. Every exertion to meet it only tightens the text, like a rope, around the neck of the belief in the historical Jesus. Our desire, in engaging in this argument, is to turn the thought and love of the world from a mythical being, to humanity, which is both real and present.

On page 22 of *The Debate,* we say: "St. Paul tells us that he lived in Jerusalem at a time when Jesus must have been holding the attention of the city; yet he never met him." To this the clergyman replies:

"Paul tells us nothing of the kind. In a speech which is put into the mouth of Paul"--*put into the mouth of Paul!* Is this another instance of forgery? John did not write the epistles, and Paul's speech in the Book of Acts was put into his mouth! Will the clergyman tell us which parts of the bible are *not* invented?

Let us make a remark: The church people blame us for not believing in the trustworthiness of the bible; but when we reply that if the bible is trustworthy, then Paul must have been in Jerusalem with Jesus, and John admits that some denied the historical Jesus, we are blamed for not knowing better than to prove anything by quoting Paul and John as if everything they said was trustworthy.

In other words, only those passages in the bible are authentic which the clergy quote; those which the rationalists quote are spurious. In the meantime, the authentic as well as the spurious passages together compose the churches' *Word of God*.

IV

In a letter of protest to Mr. Mangasarian, Rabbi Hirsch, of this city, asks: "Was it right for you to assume that I was correctly reported by the *News?*" After stating what he had said in his interview with the reporter, the Rabbi continues: "But said I to the reporter all these possible allusions do not prove that Jesus existed....You see in reality I agreed with you. I personally believe Jesus lived. But I have no proof for this beyond my feeling that the movement with which the name is associated could even for Paul not have taken its nomenclature without a personal substratum. But, and this I told the reporter also, this does not prove that the Jesus of the Gospels is historical." Rabbi Hirsch writes in this same letter that he did not say Jesus was mentioned in the Rabbinical Books. The News reports the Rabbi as saying, "But we know through the Rabbinical Books that Jesus lived."

A committee from our Society waited on the editor of the *Daily News* for an explanation. The editor promised to locate the responsibility for the contradiction.

As the report in the *News* was allowed to stand for four days without correction, and as Rabbi Hirsch did not even privately, by letter or by phone, disclaim responsibility for the article, to Mr. Mangasarian, the latter claims he was justified in assuming that the published report was reliable. But it is with pleasure that the Independent Religious Society gives Rabbi Hirsch this opportunity to explain his position. We hope he will also let us know whether he said to the reporter: "I do not believe in Mr. Mangasarian's argument that Christianity has inspired massacres, wars and inquisitions. It is a stock argument and not to the point." This is extraordinary; and as the Rabbi does not question the statement, we infer that it is a correct report of what he said. Though we have room for only one quotation from the Jewish-Christian Scriptures, it will be enough to show the relation of religion to persecution:

"And thou shalt consume all the people which the Lord, thy God, shall deliver thee; thine eye shall have no pity upon them."

Why were women put to death as witches? Why were Quakers hanged? For what "economic and political reasons," which the Rabbi thinks are responsible for persecution, was the blind Derby girl who doubted the Real Presence, burned alive at the age of twenty-two?

V

The Rev. W. E. Barton, of Oak Park, is one of the ablest Congregational ministers in the West. He has recently expressed himself on the Mangasarian-Crapsey Debate. Let us hear what he has to say on the historicity of Jesus.

The Reverend gentleman begins by an uncompromising denial of our statements, and ends by virtually admitting all that we contend for. This morning we will write of his denials; next Sunday, of his admissions.

"Mr. Mangasarian," says Dr. Barton, "has not given evidence of his skill as a logician or of his accuracy in the use of history." Then he proceeds to apologize, in a way, for the character of his reply to our argument, by saying that "Mr. Mangasarian's arguments, fortunately, do not require to be taken very seriously, for they are not in themselves serious."

Notwithstanding this protest, Dr. Barton proceeds to do his best to reply to our position.

In *The Debate* we call attention to the fact that according to the New Testament, Paul was in Jerusalem when Jesus was teaching and performing his miracles there. Yet Paul never seems to have met Jesus, or to have heard of his teachings or miracles. To this Dr. Barton replies: "We cannot know and are not bound to explain where Paul was on the few occasions when Jesus publicly visited Jerusalem."

The above reply, we are compelled to say, much to our regret, is not even honest. Without actually telling any untruths, it suggests indirectly two falsehoods: First, that Jesus was not much in Jerusalem--that he was there only on a few occasions; and that, therefore, it is not strange that Paul did not see him or hear of his preaching or miracles; and second, that Paul was absent from the city when Jesus was there. The question is not how often Jesus visited Jerusalem, but how conspicuous was the part he played there. He may have visited Jerusalem only once in all his life, yet if he preached there daily in the synagogues; if he performed great miracles there; if he marched through the streets followed by the palm-waving multitude shouting **Hosanna,** etc.; if he attacked the high-priest and the pharisees there, to which latter class Paul belonged; and if he was arrested, tried and publicly executed there; and if his teaching stirred the city from center to circumference,--it would not be honest to intimate that the "few" times Jesus visited Jerusalem, Paul was engaged elsewhere.

The Reverend debater attempts to belittle the Jerusalem career of Jesus, by suggesting that he was not there much, when according to the Gospels, it was in that city that his ministry began and culminated.

Again, to our argument that Paul never refers to any of the teachings of Jesus, the Reverend replies: "Nor is it of consequence that Paul **seldom** quotes the words of Jesus." **"Seldom"**---would imply that Paul quotes Jesus sometimes. We say Paul gives not a single quotation to prove that he knew of a teaching Jesus. He had heard of a crucified, risen, Christ--one who had also instituted a bread and wine supper, but of Jesus as a **teacher** and of his **teaching,** Paul is absolutely ignorant.

But by saying "Paul **seldom** quotes Jesus," Dr. Barton tries to produce the impression that Paul quotes Jesus, though not very often, which is not true. There is not a single miracle, parable or moral teaching attributed to Jesus in the Gospels of which Paul seems to possess any knowledge whatever.

Nor is it true that it is of no consequence that "Paul seldom quotes the words of Jesus." For it proves that the Gospel Jesus was unknown to Paul, and that he was created at a later date.

Once more; we say that the only Jesus Paul knew was the one he met in a trance on his way to Damascus. To this the pastor of the First Congregational Church of Oak Park replies in the same we-do-not-care- to-explain style. He says: "Nor is it of consequence that Paul values comparatively lightly, having known him in the flesh."

The words "Paul valued comparatively lightly" are as misleading as the words "Paul **seldom** quotes Jesus." Paul **never** quotes Jesus' teachings, and he **never** met Jesus in the flesh. The clergyman's words, however, convey the impression that Paul knew Jesus in the flesh, but he valued that, knowledge "comparatively lightly," that is to say, he did not think much of it. And Dr. Barton is one of the foremost divines of the country.

And now about his admissions:

VI

I. "The Gospels, by whomever written," says the clergyman, "are reliable." By *whomever* written! After two thousand years, it is still uncertain to whom we are indebted for the story of Jesus. What, in Dr. Barton's opinion, could have influenced the framers of the life of Jesus to suppress their identity? And why does not the church instead of printing the words, "The Gospel according to Matthew or John," which is *not true,*--print, "The Gospel by *whomever* written"?

II. "At the very least, four of Paul's epistles are genuine," says the same clergyman. Only four? Paul has thirteen epistles in the bible, and of only four of them is Dr. Barton certain. What are the remaining nine doing in the Holy Bible? And which 'four' does the clergyman accept as doubtlessly "genuine?" Only yesterday all thirteen of Paul's letters were infallible, and they are so still wherever no questions are asked about them. It is only where there is intelligence and inquiry that "four of them" at least are reliable. As honesty and culture increase, the number of inspired epistles decreases. What the Americans are too enlightened to accept, the church sends to the *heathen*.

III. "It is true that early a sect grew up which....held that Jesus could not have had a body of carnal flesh; but they did not question that he had really lived." According to Dr. Barton, these early Christians did not deny that Jesus had really lived,--they only denied that *Jesus could have had a body of carnal flesh*. We wonder how many kinds of flesh there are according to Dr. Barton. Moreover, does not the bible teach that Jesus was tempted in all things, and was a man of like passions, as ourselves? The good man controls his appetites and passions, but his flesh is not any different from anybody else's. If Jesus did not have a body like ours, then he did not exist as a human being. Our point is, that if the New Testament is reliable, in the time of the apostles themselves, the Gnostics, an influential body of Christians, denied that Jesus was any more than an imaginary existence. "But," pleads the clergyman, "these sects believed that Jesus was real, though not carnal flesh." What kind of flesh was he then? If by *carnal* the Gnostics meant 'sensual,' then, the apostles in denouncing them for rejecting a carnal Jesus, must have held that Jesus was carnal or sensual. How does the Reverend Barton like the conclusion to which his own reasoning leads him?

IV. "It is true that there were literary fictions in the age following the apostles." This admission is in answer to the charge that even in the first centuries the Christians were compelled to resort to forgery to prove the historicity of Jesus. The doctor admits the charge, except that he calls it by another name. The difference between fiction and forgery is this: the former is, what it claims to be; the latter is a lie parading as a truth. Fiction is honest because it does not try to deceive. Forgery is dishonest because its object is to deceive. If the Gospel was a novel, no one would object to its mythology, but pretending to be historical, it must square its claims with the facts, or be branded as a forgery.

V. "We may not have the precise words Jesus uttered; the portrait may be colored;....tradition may have had its influence; but Jesus was real." A most remarkable admission from a clerical! It concedes all that higher criticism contends for. We are not sure either of Jesus' words or of his character, intimates the Reverend preacher. Precisely.

In commenting on our remark that in the eighth century "Pope Hadrian called upon the Christian world to think of Jesus as a man," Dr. Barton replies with considerable temper: "To date people's right to think of Jesus as a man from that decree is not to be characterized by any polite term." Our neighbor, in the first place, misquotes us in his haste. We never presumed to deny anyone the right to think of Jesus what he pleased, before or after the eighth century. (*The Debate,* p. 28.) We were calling attention to Pope Hadrian's order to replace the lamb on the cross by the figure of a man. But by what *polite* language is the conduct of the Christian church--which to this day prints in its bibles "Translated from the Original Greek," when no *original* manuscripts are in existence--to be characterized?

Dr. Barton's efforts to save his creed remind us of the Japanese proverb: "It is no use mending the lid, if the pot be broken."

VII

The most remarkable clerical effort thus far, which *The Mangasarian- Crapsey Debate* has called forth, is that of the Rev. E. V. Shayler, rector of Grace Episcopal Church of Oak Park.

"In answer to your query, which I received, I beg to give the following statement. Facts, not theories. The date of your own letter 1908 tells what? 1908 years after what? The looking forward of the world to Him."

Rev. Shayler has an original way of proving the historicity of Jesus. Every time we date our letters, suggests the clergyman, we prove that Jesus lived. The ancient Greeks reckoned time by the Olympiads, which fact, according to this interesting clergyman, ought to prove that the Olympic games were instituted by the God Heracles or Hercules, son of Zeus; the Roman Chronology began with the building of Rome by Romulus, which by the same reasoning would prove that Romulus and Remus, born of Mars, and nursed by a she-wolf, are historical.

Rev. Shayler has forgotten that the Christian era was not introduced into Europe until the sixth century, and Dionysius, the monkish author of the era, did not compute time from the birth of Jesus, but from the day on which the Virgin Mary met an angel from heaven. This date prevailed in many countries until 1745. Would the date on a letter prove that an angel appeared to Mary and hailed her as the future Mother of God? According to this clergyman, scientists, instead of studying the crust of the earth and making geological investigations to ascertain the probable age of the earth, ought to look at the date in the margin of the bible which tells exactly the world's age.

Rev. Shayler continues: "The places where he was born, labored and died are still extant, and have no value apart from such testimony."

While this is amusing, we are going to deny ourselves the pleasure of laughing at it; we will do our best to give it a serious answer. If the existence of such a country as Palestine proves that Jesus is real, the existence of Switzerland must prove that William Tell is historical; and the existence of an Athens must prove that Athene and Apollo really lived; and from the fact that there is an England, Rev. Shayler would prove that Robin Hood and his band really lived in 1160.

The Reverend knows of another 'fact' which he thinks proves Jesus without a doubt:

"A line of apostles and bishops coming right down from him by his appointment to Anderson of Chicago," shows that Jesus is historical. It does, but only to Episcopalians. The Catholics and the other sects do not believe that Anderson is a descendant of Jesus. Did the priests of Baal or Moloch prove that these beings existed?

The Reverend has another argument:

"The Christian Church--when, why and how did it begin?" Which Christian church, brother? Your own church began with Henry the Eighth in 1534, with persecution and murder, when the king, his hands wet with the blood of his own wives and ministers, made himself the supreme head of the church in England. The Methodist church began with John Wesley not much over a hundred years ago; the Presbyterian church began with John Calvin who burned his guest on a slow fire in Geneva about three hundred years ago; and the Lutheran church began with Martin Luther in the sixteenth century, the man who said over his own signature: "It was I, Martin Luther, who slew all the peasants in the Peasants War, for I commanded them to be slaughtered....But I throw the responsibility on our Lord God who instructed me to give this order;" and the Roman Catholic church, the parent of the smaller churches--all chips from the same block--began its real career with the first Christian Emperor, Constantine, who hanged his father-in- law, strangled his brother-in-law, murdered his nephew, beheaded his eldest son, and killed his wife. Gibbon writes of Constantine that "the same year of his reign in which he convened the council of Nice was polluted by the execution, or rather murder, of his eldest son."

But our clerical neighbor from Oak Park has one more argument: "Why is Sunday observed instead of Saturday?" Well, why? Sun-day is the day of the Sun, whose glorious existence in the lovely heavens over our heads has never been doubted; it was the day which the Pagans dedicated to the Sun. *Sunday* existed before the Jesus story was known,--the anniversary of whose supposed resurrection falls in March one year, and in April another. If Jesus rose at all, he rose on a certain day, and the apostles must have known the date. Why then is there a different date every year?

Rev. Shayler concludes: "Haven't time to go deeper now," and he intimates that to deny his 'facts' is either to be a fool or a "liar." We will not comment on this. We are interested in arguments, not in epithets.

VIII

One of our Sunday programs, the other day, found its way into a church. It went farther; it made its appearance in the pulpit.

"In my hand I hold the notice of a publication bearing the title *Is Jesus a Myth?"* said Dr. Boyle. "This, too, just as though Paul never bore testimony."

This gave the clergyman a splendid opportunity to present in clear and convincing form the evidence for the reality of Jesus. But one thing prevented him:-- the lack of evidence.

Therefore, after announcing the subject, he dismissed it, by remarking that Paul's testimony was enough.

The Rev. Morton Culver Hartzell, in a letter, offers the same argument. "Let Mr. Mangasarian first disprove Paul," he writes. The argument in a nutshell is this: Jesus is historical because he is guaranteed by Paul.

But *who* guarantees Paul?

Aside from the fact that the Jesus of Paul is essentially a different Jesus from the gospel Jesus there still remains the question, Who is Paul? Let us see how much the church scholars themselves know about Paul:

"The place and manner and occasion of his death are not *less uncertain* than the facts of his later life...The chronology of the rest of his life is as uncertain...We have no means of knowing when he was born, or how long he lived, or at what dates the several events of his life took place."

Referring to the epistles of Paul, the same authority says: "The chief of these preliminary questions is the genuineness of the epistles bearing Paul's name, which *if they be his*"--yes, IF--

The Christian scholar whose article on Paul is printed in the *Britannica*, and from which we are now quoting, gives further expression to this uncertainty by adding that certain of Paul's epistles "have given rise to disputes which cannot easily be settled in the absence of collateral evidence...The pastoral epistles...have given rise to still graver questions, and are probably even *less* defensible."

Let the reader remember that the above is not from a rationalist, but from the Rev. Edwin Hatch, D. D., Vice-Principal, St. Mary Hall, Oxford, England.

Were we disposed to quote rationalist authorities, the argument against Paul would be far more decisive. But we are satisfied to rest the case on orthodox admissions alone.

The strongest argument then of clergymen who have attempted an answer to our position is something like this:

Jesus is historical because a man by the name of Paul says so, though we do not know much about Paul.

It is just such evidence as the above that led Prof. Goldwin Smith to exclaim: "Jesus has flown. I believe the legend of Jesus was made by many minds working under a great religious impulse--one man adding a parable, another an exhortation, another a miracle story;"--and George Eliot to write: "The materials for a real life of Christ do not exist."

In the effort to untie the Jesus-knot by Paul, the church has increased the number of knots to two. In other words, the church has proceeded on the theory that two uncertainties make a certainty.

We promised to square also with the facts of history our statement that the chief concern of the church, Jewish, Christian, or Mohammedan, is not righteousness, but orthodoxy.

IX

Speaking in this city, Rev. W. H. Wray Boyle of Lake Forest, declared that unbelief was responsible for the worst crimes in history. He mentioned the placing.

--"of a nude woman on a pedestal in the city of Paris.

--"the assassination of William McKinley.

--"The same unbelief sent a murderer down the isle of a church in Denver to pluck the symbol of the sacrament from the hands of a priest and slay him at the altar."

The story of a "nude woman," etc., is pure fiction, and that the two murders were caused by unbelief is mere assumption. To help his creed, the preacher resorts to fable. We shall prove our position by quoting *facts*:

I. HYPATIA [Note: See Author's, The Martyrdom of Hypatia.] was dragged into a Christian church by monks in Alexandria, and before the altar she was stripped of her clothing and cut in pieces with oyster shells, and murdered. Her innocent blood stained the hands of the clergy, who also handle the Holy Sacraments. She was murdered not by a crazed individual but by the orders of the bishop of Alexandria. How does the true story of Hypatia compare with the fable of "a nude woman placed on a pedestal in the city of Paris?" The Reverend must answer, or never tell an untruth again.

Hypatia was murdered in church, and by the clergy, because she was not orthodox.

II. POLTROT, the Protestant, in the 16th century assassinated Francois, the Catholic duke of Guise, in France, and the leaders of the church, instead of disclaiming responsibility for the act, publicly praised the assassin, and Theodore Beza, the colleague of Calvin, promised him a crown in heaven. (*De l'etat etc, P. 82.* Quoted by Jules Simon.)

III. JAMES CLEMENT, a Catholic, assassinated Henry III. For this act the clergy placed his portrait on the altar in the churches between two great lighted candlesticks. Because he had killed a heretic prince, the Catholics presented the assassin's mother with a purse. (*Esprit de la Ligue I. III. P. 14.*)

If it was unbelief that inspired the murder of McKinley, what inspired the assassins of Hypatia and Henry III?

We read in the Bible that Gen. Sisera, a heathen, having lost a battle, begged for shelter at the tent of Jael, a friendly woman, but of the Bible faith. Jael assured the unfortunate stranger that he was safe in her tent. The tired warrior fell asleep from great weariness. Then Jael picked a tent-peg and with a hammer in her hand "walked softly unto him, and smote the nail into his temples, and fastened it into the ground...So he died."

The BIBLE calls this assassin "blessed above women." (*Judge IV. 18, etc.*) She had killed a heretic.

In each of the instances given above, the assassin is honored because he committed murder in the interest of the faith. We ask this clergyman and his colleagues who are only too anxious to charge every act of violence to unbelief in their creeds--What about the crimes of **believers**?

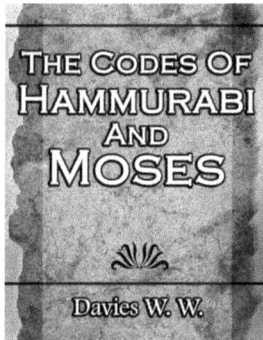

The Codes Of Hammurabi And Moses
W. W. Davies

QTY

The discovery of the Hammurabi Code is one of the greatest achievements of archaeology, and is of paramount interest, not only to the student of the Bible, but also to all those interested in ancient history...

Religion   **ISBN: *1-59462-338-4***   **Pages:132**

MSRP $12.95

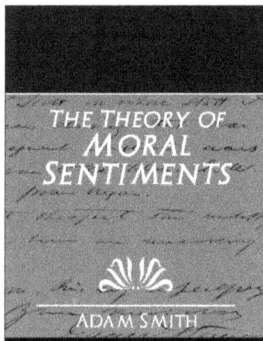

The Theory of Moral Sentiments
Adam Smith

QTY

This work from 1749. contains original theories of conscience amd moral judgment and it is the foundation for systemof morals.

Philosophy ISBN: *1-59462-777-0*   **Pages:536**

MSRP $19.95

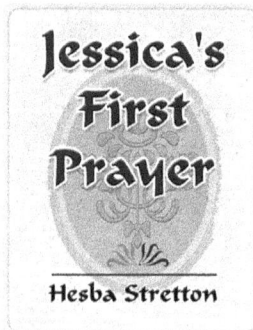

Jessica's First Prayer
Hesba Stretton

QTY

In a screened and secluded corner of one of the many railway-bridges which span the streets of London there could be seen a few years ago, from five o'clock every morning until half past eight, a tidily set-out coffee-stall, consisting of a trestle and board, upon which stood two large tin cans, with a small fire of charcoal burning under each so as to keep the coffee boiling during the early hours of the morning when the work-people were thronging into the city on their way to their daily toil...

Pages:84

Childrens   ISBN: *1-59462-373-2*   *MSRP $9.95*

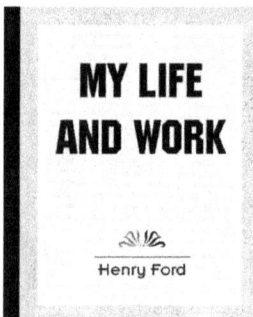

My Life and Work
Henry Ford

QTY

Henry Ford revolutionized the world with his implementation of mass production for the Model T automobile. Gain valuable business insight into his life and work with his own auto-biography... "We have only started on our development of our country we have not as yet, with all our talk of wonderful progress, done more than scratch the surface. The progress has been wonderful enough but..."

Pages:300

Biographies/   ISBN: *1-59462-198-5*   *MSRP $21.95*

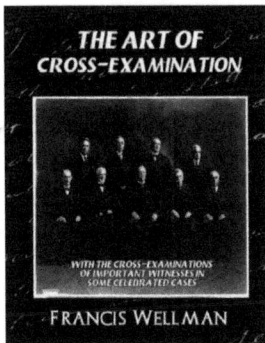

The Art of Cross-Examination
Francis Wellman

QTY

I presume it is the experience of every author, after his first book is published upon an important subject, to be almost overwhelmed with a wealth of ideas and illustrations which could readily have been included in his book, and which to his own mind, at least, seem to make a second edition inevitable. Such certainly was the case with me; and when the first edition had reached its sixth impression in five months, I rejoiced to learn that it seemed to my publishers that the book had met with a sufficiently favorable reception to justify a second and considerably enlarged edition. ..

Pages:412

Reference   **ISBN: *1-59462-647-2***   *MSRP $19.95*

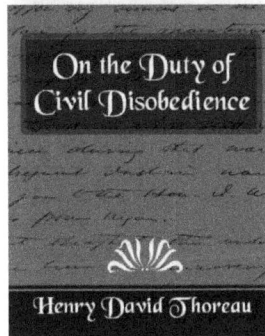

On the Duty of Civil Disobedience
Henry David Thoreau

QTY

Thoreau wrote his famous essay, On the Duty of Civil Disobedience, as a protest against an unjust but popular war and the immoral but popular institution of slave-owning. He did more than write—he declined to pay his taxes, and was hauled off to gaol in consequence. Who can say how much this refusal of his hastened the end of the war and of slavery ?

Law   **ISBN: *1-59462-747-9***   **Pages:48**

MSRP $7.45

Dream Psychology Psychoanalysis for Beginners
Sigmund Freud

QTY

Sigmund Freud, born Sigismund Schlomo Freud (May 6, 1856 - September 23, 1939), was a Jewish-Austrian neurologist and psychiatrist who co-founded the psychoanalytic school of psychology. Freud is best known for his theories of the unconscious mind, especially involving the mechanism of repression; his redefinition of sexual desire as mobile and directed towards a wide variety of objects; and his therapeutic techniques, especially his understanding of transference in the therapeutic relationship and the presumed value of dreams as sources of insight into unconscious desires.

Pages:196

Psychology   **ISBN: *1-59462-905-6***   *MSRP $15.45*

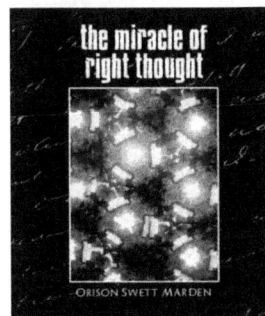

The Miracle of Right Thought
Orison Swett Marden

QTY

Believe with all of your heart that you will do what you were made to do. When the mind has once formed the habit of holding cheerful, happy, prosperous pictures, it will not be easy to form the opposite habit. It does not matter how improbable or how far away this realization may see, or how dark the prospects may be, if we visualize them as best we can, as vividly as possible, hold tenaciously to them and vigorously struggle to attain them, they will gradually become actualized, realized in the life. But a desire, a longing without endeavor, a yearning abandoned or held indifferently will vanish without realization.

Pages:360

Self Help   **ISBN: *1-59462-644-8***   *MSRP $25.45*

QTY

☐ **The Rosicrucian Cosmo-Conception Mystic Christianity** by *Max Heindel*   ISBN: *1-59462-188-8* **$38.95**
The Rosicrucian Cosmo-conception is not dogmatic, neither does it appeal to any other authority than the reason of the student. It is: not controversial, but is: sent forth in, the hope that it may help to clear...   New Age/Religion Pages 646

☐ **Abandonment To Divine Providence** by *Jean-Pierre de Caussade*   ISBN: *1-59462-228-0* **$25.95**
"The Rev. Jean Pierre de Caussade was one of the most remarkable spiritual writers of the Society of Jesus in France in the 18th Century. His death took place at Toulouse in 1751. His works have gone through many editions and have been republished...   Inspirational/Religion Pages 400

☐ **Mental Chemistry** by *Charles Haanel*   ISBN: *1-59462-192-6* **$23.95**
Mental Chemistry allows the change of material conditions by combining and appropriately utilizing the power of the mind. Much like applied chemistry creates something new and unique out of careful combinations of chemicals the mastery of mental chemistry...   New Age Pages 354

☐ **The Letters of Robert Browning and Elizabeth Barret Barrett 1845-1846 vol II**   ISBN: *1-59462-193-4* **$35.95**
by *Robert Browning and Elizabeth Barrett*   Biographies Pages 596

☐ **Gleanings In Genesis (volume I)** by *Arthur W. Pink*   ISBN: *1-59462-130-6* **$27.45**
Appropriately has Genesis been termed "the seed plot of the Bible" for in it we have, in germ form, almost all of the great doctrines which are afterwards fully developed in the books of Scripture which follow...   Religion/Inspirational Pages 420

☐ **The Master Key** by *L. W. de Laurence*   ISBN: *1-59462-001-6* **$30.95**
In no branch of human knowledge has there been a more lively increase of the spirit of research during the past few years than in the study of Psychology, Concentration and Mental Discipline. The requests for authentic lessons in Thought Control, Mental Discipline and...   New Age/Business Pages 422

☐ **The Lesser Key Of Solomon Goetia** by *L. W. de Laurence*   ISBN: *1-59462-092-X* **$9.95**
This translation of the first book of the "Lernegton" which is now for the first time made accessible to students of Talismanic Magic was done, after careful collation and edition, from numerous Ancient Manuscripts in Hebrew, Latin, and French...   New Age/Occult Pages 92

☐ **Rubaiyat Of Omar Khayyam** by *Edward Fitzgerald*   ISBN:*1-59462-332-5* **$13.95**
Edward Fitzgerald, whom the world has already learned, in spite of his own efforts to remain within the shadow of anonymity, to look upon as one of the rarest poets of the century, was born at Bredfield, in Suffolk, on the 31st of March, 1809. He was the third son of John Purcell...   Music Pages 172

☐ **Ancient Law** by *Henry Maine*   ISBN: *1-59462-128-4* **$29.95**
The chief object of the following pages is to indicate some of the earliest ideas of mankind, as they are reflected in Ancient Law, and to point out the relation of those ideas to modern thought.   Religion/History Pages 452

☐ **Far-Away Stories** by *William J. Locke*   ISBN: *1-59462-129-2* **$19.45**
"Good wine needs no bush," but a collection of mixed vintages does. And this book is just such a collection. Some of the stories I do not want to remain buried for ever in the museum files of dead magazine-numbers an author's not unpardonable vanity..."   Fiction Pages 272

☐ **Life of David Crockett** by *David Crockett*   ISBN: *1-59462-250-7* **$27.45**
"Colonel David Crockett was one of the most remarkable men of the times in which he lived. Born in humble life, but gifted with a strong will, an indomitable courage, and unremitting perseverance...   Biographies/New Age Pages 424

☐ **Lip-Reading** by *Edward Nitchie*   ISBN: *1-59462-206-X* **$25.95**
Edward B. Nitchie, founder of the New York School for the Hard of Hearing, now the Nitchie School of Lip-Reading, Inc, wrote "LIP-READING Principles and Practice". The development and perfecting of this meritorious work on lip-reading was an undertaking...   How-to Pages 400

☐ **A Handbook of Suggestive Therapeutics, Applied Hypnotism, Psychic Science**   ISBN: *1-59462-214-0* **$24.95**
by *Henry Munro*   Health/New Age/Health/Self-help Pages 376

☐ **A Doll's House: and Two Other Plays** by *Henrik Ibsen*   ISBN: *1-59462-112-8* **$19.95**
Henrik Ibsen created this classic when in revolutionary 1848 Rome. Introducing some striking concepts in playwriting for the realist genre, this play has been studied the world over.   Fiction/Classics/Plays 308

☐ **The Light of Asia** by *sir Edwin Arnold*   ISBN: *1-59462-204-3* **$13.95**
In this poetic masterpiece, Edwin Arnold describes the life and teachings of Buddha. The man who was to become known as Buddha to the world was born as Prince Gautama of India but he rejected the worldly riches and abandoned the reigns of power when...   Religion/History/Biographies Pages 170

☐ **The Complete Works of Guy de Maupassant** by *Guy de Maupassant*   ISBN: *1-59462-157-8* **$16.95**
"For days and days, nights and nights, I had dreamed of that first kiss which was to consecrate our engagement, and I knew not on what spot I should put my lips..."   Fiction/Classics Pages 240

☐ **The Art of Cross-Examination** by *Francis L. Wellman*   ISBN: *1-59462-309-0* **$26.95**
Written by a renowned trial lawyer, Wellman imparts his experience and uses case studies to explain how to use psychology to extract desired information through questioning.   How-to/Science/Reference Pages 408

☐ **Answered or Unanswered?** by *Louisa Vaughan*   ISBN: *1-59462-248-5* **$10.95**
Miracles of Faith in China   Religion Pages 112

☐ **The Edinburgh Lectures on Mental Science (1909)** by *Thomas*   ISBN: *1-59462-008-3* **$11.95**
This book contains the substance of a course of lectures recently given by the writer in the Queen Street Hall, Edinburgh. Its purpose is to indicate the Natural Principles governing the relation between Mental Action and Material Conditions...   New Age/Psychology Pages 148

☐ **Ayesha** by *H. Rider Haggard*   ISBN: *1-59462-301-5* **$24.95**
Verily and indeed it is the unexpected that happens! Probably if there was one person upon the earth from whom the Editor of this, and of a certain previous history, did not expect to hear again...   Classics Pages 380

☐ **Ayala's Angel** by *Anthony Trollope*   ISBN: *1-59462-352-X* **$29.95**
The two girls were both pretty, but Lucy who was twenty-one who supposed to be simple and comparatively unattractive, whereas Ayala was credited, as her Bombwhat romantic name might show, with poetic charm and a taste for romance. Ayala when her father died was nineteen...   Fiction Pages 484

☐ **The American Commonwealth** by *James Bryce*   ISBN: *1-59462-286-8* **$34.45**
An interpretation of American democratic political theory. It examines political mechanics and society from the perspective of Scotsman James Bryce   Politics Pages 572

☐ **Stories of the Pilgrims** by *Margaret P. Pumphrey*   ISBN: *1-59462-116-0* **$17.95**
This book explores pilgrims religious oppression in England as well as their escape to Holland and eventual crossing to America on the Mayflower, and their early days in New England...   History Pages 268

QTY

The Fasting Cure *by Sinclair Upton*　　ISBN: *1-59462-222-1*　**$13.95**
In the Cosmopolitan Magazine for May, 1910, and in the Contemporary Review (London) for April, 1910, I published an article dealing with my experiences in fasting. I have written a great many magazine articles, but never one which attracted so much attention... New Age/Self Help/Health Pages 164

Hebrew Astrology *by Sepharial*　　ISBN: *1-59462-308-2*　**$13.45**
In these days of advanced thinking it is a matter of common observation that we have left many of the old landmarks behind and that we are now pressing forward to greater heights and to a wider horizon than that which represented the mind-content of our progenitors... Astrology Pages 144

Thought Vibration or The Law of Attraction in the Thought World　　ISBN: *1-59462-127-6*　**$12.95**

by William Walker Atkinson　　Psychology/Religion Pages 144

Optimism *by Helen Keller*　　ISBN: *1-59462-108-X*　**$15.95**
Helen Keller was blind, deaf, and mute since 19 months old, yet famously learned how to overcome these handicaps, communicate with the world, and spread her lectures promoting optimism. An inspiring read for everyone... Biographies/Inspirational Pages 84

Sara Crewe *by Frances Burnett*　　ISBN: *1-59462-360-0*　**$9.45**
In the first place, Miss Minchin lived in London. Her home was a large, dull, tall one, in a large, dull square, where all the houses were alike, and all the sparrows were alike, and where all the door-knockers made the same heavy sound... Childrens/Classic Pages 88

The Autobiography of Benjamin Franklin *by Benjamin Franklin*　　ISBN: *1-59462-135-7*　**$24.95**
The Autobiography of Benjamin Franklin has probably been more extensively read than any other American historical work, and no other book of its kind has had such ups and downs of fortune. Franklin lived for many years in England, where he was agent... Biographies/History Pages 332

Name	
Email	
Telephone	
Address	
City, State ZIP	

☐ **Credit Card**　　☐ **Check / Money Order**

Credit Card Number	
Expiration Date	
Signature	

Please Mail to:　Book Jungle
PO Box 2226
Champaign, IL 61825
or Fax to:　　630-214-0564

ORDERING INFORMATION

web*: www.bookjungle.com*
email*: sales@bookjungle.com*
fax*: 630-214-0564*
mail*: Book Jungle PO Box 2226 Champaign, IL 61825*
or PayPal *to sales@bookjungle.com*

Please contact us for bulk discounts

DIRECT-ORDER TERMS

**20% Discount if You Order
Two or More Books**
Free Domestic Shipping!
Accepted: Master Card, Visa,
Discover, American Express

www.ingramcontent.com/pod-product-compliance
Lightning Source LLC
Chambersburg PA
CBHW050353100426
42739CB00015BB/3386